Writing about Music

WRITING
ABOUT
MUSIC

A Style Book for Reports and Theses

By DEMAR IRVINE

Second edition, revised and enlarged

Seattle and London
UNIVERSITY OF WASHINGTON PRESS

Reading maketh a full man,
conference a ready man,
and writing an exact man.

FRANCIS BACON

PREFACE

Writing about Music first appeared in 1956, without the luxury of a preface, and with 102 rules. For the present edition the material has undergone a thorough overhauling. Some attempt has been made to answer questions arising out of the use of the earlier edition. It is hoped that the present organization into major sections will make the book easier to use. In the new arrangement, Part One is devoted to details of style in the typescript, while Part Two (with much new material) attempts to provide helpful suggestions for the improvement of literary style.

Whoever becomes involved with music, whether as student, amateur, or professional, is bound sooner or later to want to discuss this fascinating art. Reading about composers, performers, and various musical subjects improves our knowledge, and certainly conversation with our friends offers a ready forum for exchanges of opinion. But for exactitude and permanence of expression there is nothing quite like *writing* about one's subject, as Francis Bacon so epigrammatically pointed out long ago.

This book is obviously intended primarily for students of music. There are no age limits restricting one's status as "student," nor does one ever really reach a saturation point where knowledge is concerned. The whole exciting paradox of life is that the more we know, the more new avenues are opened for further discovery. In the old days, when people kept extensive diaries and wrote long letters to one another, perhaps much more of each individual's personal development and intellectual growth got reduced to writing. Nowadays, we have to force ourselves just a little to take our pen in hand.

Students of music are typically too busy with *music* to do much writing about it. There is no reason, though, why we cannot learn to be bilingual: to speak directly music's own language, and also to express our thoughts and ideas in words. This latter activity brings its own special kind of satisfaction, a refreshing change of pace from always practicing, performing, composing, or for that matter just listening.

Where writing is concerned, it is often a question of overcoming inertia and *getting started*. We all have excellent ideas from time to time, but we tend to be, let us say, too lazy to put them down. With a little persistent concentration and effort it is surprising how soon one can begin to look upon one's literary products with a certain pride. The secret is to start with the techniques. It is the acquisition of technical skill that gives us a command over what we are doing. An analogy: for good progress in piano playing, is it not best to devote some attention to scales, exercises, and études? Does not the building up of technique open doors to accomplishment of broader goals, such as artistic performance?

To acquire technical skill, it is best to begin with a great many very short papers, on a variety of subjects. (Compare rule 209.) It is comforting if one can have a sympathetic critic looking over one's shoulder. As with any form of communication, we need an audience in order to judge how well we are getting across. Still, there is much that can be accomplished in quiet solitude, and it is here that the present manual is intended to be helpful.

The various "rules" (so called for convenience, not because they are inflexible laws) are consecutively numbered for ready reference and cross reference. It is recommended that they be taken as one-a-day capsules—as a kind of supplement to your main diet, which ought to consist of the best books you can find and read on musical subjects that interest you. A gulp here, a gulp there, taken with reasonable frequency, is guaranteed to build up iron-poor literary blood.

Writing is never exactly *easy*. There is ample testimony to that by many of the best writers, who have been known to struggle for long hours over a single paragraph. In other words, there is always room for improvement. But the student who takes time to think consciously about principles, and to practice techniques, will learn to make his writing seem fluent and carry conviction.

D. I.

CONTENTS

Part One: Style in the Typescript

Part Two: Writing Skills

PART ONE

Style in the Typescript

PRELUDE

"Style" is a technical term used in the publications field to mean a consistent and acceptable manner of dealing with details of typography, spelling, punctuation, documentation, and the like, in books and periodicals. The word "form" is sometimes used in place of "style."

Handwritten or typewritten matter intended to be set up in type and printed is known as "copy." Complete copy for a book or article, as provided by the author, is usually typewritten, and is called by publishers a "manuscript."

There are many different styles, and these styles, like fashions in general, tend to change over periods of time. To assist authors in preparing manuscripts, publishing concerns or individuals may provide manuals of style, style sheets, or form books, ranging in size from mere leaflets to respectable volumes.

An author preparing a manuscript for publication in a specific periodical, or by a specific book publisher, should be guided in matters of style by the editor in charge of publication. It may save time and embarrassment to address a preliminary inquiry to the editor, who may provide an abridged style sheet or other helpful advice. For excellent general advice consult the *MLA Style Sheet* and the University of Chicago Press *Manual of Style*, which are described in the Bibliography at the end of this book.

The present Style Book is designed primarily as a guide for the final form of a typewritten report, term paper, or thesis not being prepared for immediate publication. Such a document will be referred to hereafter as a "typescript." It is assumed that, in most instances, the typescript will represent the ultimate and permanent shape of the paper. The rules here given will therefore serve the convenience of potential readers rather than the convenience of a typesetter. For example: It is recommended that footnotes be single spaced and placed at the bottom of each page, rather than collected at the end double spaced.

The printed book, to which the reader is normally accustomed, serves as a general model for style in the typescript. However, in view of the typewriter's limitations, certain conventions are generally accepted for purposes of adapting book style to typescripts. These are fully covered below, and the beginner should conform closely to the specifications given. The more experienced author-typist, on the other hand, may find in printed books and articles many helpful hints on stylistic details which he can adapt to the typescript. One must be careful, however, to avoid (1) bringing together inconsistent procedures from different models, or (2) adopting from older publications stylistic devices that are now out of fashion.

The rules here given are not necessarily the only acceptable rules. For any given rule one or more variants can usually be found. To avoid tempting the beginner into inconsistencies, most of the variants have been omitted here. The most important rule of all is that, whatever the style adopted, the author must remain consistent within his own practice.

Most normal operations in preparing typescript have been covered. Where problems arise that are not provided for, common sense will usually find an acceptable solution. If the problem persists, recourse may be had to some more elaborate form book, or to the personal advice of someone experienced in these matters.

I

THE DRAFT

1 "Draftsmanship"

Very few writers (including professionals) are able to attain the desired results in a single writing. It is to be expected that any prose communication will have to go through several successive revisions before it becomes presentable. Let your motto be: Spare the drafts and spoil the report! A common fault is to assume that the first version, typed out in a burst of supposed inspiration, will represent the writer's best effort, or that it will be read with any pleasure by anyone else.

2 The outline

Assuming that the research is completed, or at least well under way, select a title (rule 179), and work up in outline form a plan of presentation that is logical and convincing. An effective outline is the key to successful organization of a report. Professors will often refuse to supervise the writing of a thesis until the student has submitted an "outline" demonstrating a thorough grasp of the whole subject.

The chief fault of an outline is that it may leave the writer uncommitted. Key words are mentioned as subjects, but usually without predicates. Hence it may not always be clear what stand the writer intends to take.

3 The brief

As an alternative to the outline, the "brief" is recommended. A brief consists of a series of positive statements, in sentence form, representing the main flow of ideas to be presented in the report. Each sentence in a brief is roughly equivalent to a topic sentence (rule 188) governing a whole paragraph or section in the completed report. Writing the paper then becomes a matter of amplifying, explaining, and illustrating the main ideas thus succinctly stated.

To control organization, adjust and rearrange the sequence of ideas in the brief until everything falls neatly into place in the proper order.

A "brief" (precomposition) is rather like an "abstract" (post-condensation; cf. rule 170). Where a report has been so poorly organized that it requires rewriting, begin by abstracting. That is, select out the successive topic sentences or other governing statements (if there are any!), and run them together as, a test of coherence. It may be found that the defective report has no skeleton to hold it together, or that the skeleton has no convincing shape. Start afresh with a crisply worded brief, and the revised report will be vastly improved.

4 Rough draft

The first attempt to expand the outline or brief into a full-fledged report will usually take the form of a "rough draft." A rough draft is for your eyes alone, and should *never* be submitted to anyone else to read. As a private document, it may be as ragged or as neat as you like: in pencil, ink, or typewritten; on one or both sides of any kind of paper; with corrections and alterations as many as needed. However, never permit a rough draft to become so cluttered that you cannot readily make a clean and accurate copy from it.

5 First (second, third . . .) draft

For most reports and term papers, the final typescript is made directly from the rough draft. But if the writer has difficulty in controlling style—or better yet, if the proficient writer would achieve still greater proficiency—it is advisable to plan one or more clean drafts before arriving at the final typescript. With theses (which are ever so permanent, and come back to haunt us in later years), only fools rush in with a first draft where angels fear to tread with a third or fourth.

Regarding footnotes in the draft, see rule 78.

Any draft that is to be seen by others must be "fair copy"—that is, typewritten if possible (with double spacing in the main text), clean and legible, and free from excessive written-in corrections. Avoid lightweight paper (rule 11). If a draft is to be submitted simultaneously to two or three persons for criticism, make sure the carbon copies are neat (rule 136).

6   Criticisms of the draft

Theses always, term papers sometimes, and reports occasionally, need to be submitted in draft form for criticism. If there is any question about it, put the word DRAFT prominently at the top of the first page, as an invitation to the critic to mark up the copy freely. If the reader-critic is conscientious, he may:

Write corrections and insertions in pencil above the line, or in the margin, with a caret to show the exact location.

Cross out, or enclose in brackets (with a "delete" sign in the margin), material that should be removed.

? (query) in the margin those places where your wording does not communicate, or where the validity of a statement or the logic of an argument is open to debate. The query is an invitation to the writer to engage in self-analysis. But if the critic wishes to be more explicit, he may put "not clear" where you fail to communicate, "No!" where your facts or reasoning are wrong, or an occasional "Yes" or "Good" where praise is merited.

Suggest extensive rewordings or insertions on separate sheets as "Substitute A (B, C . . .)" or "Insert A (B, C . . .)." Consider supplying blank sheets along with the report for this purpose. Otherwise the critic may simply write on the backs of your typed pages.

Make marginal comments, or an extended commentary on a separate sheet. Where there is room for doubt as between a comment and a recommended wording of the text, remarks addressed to the writer may be circled in pencil. Alternatively, "Read:" or

"Put:" should make it clear that what follows is a recommended wording of the text.

If there are reasons why the reader-critic should *not* mark up your typescript, explain orally, or in an attached note, or put FAIR COPY or FINAL COPY at the top of the first page. In this case, the conscientious critic will draw up a separate report and hand it to the writer. Items or passages commented upon may be identified as "p. 2, line 6," . . . "p. 5, lines 16-23," . . . p. 8, 3rd par.," or the like. It is a courtesy to supply extra sheets of paper for this purpose.

7 Corrections in the draft

Corrections and insertions, if they are brief, may be written legibly in pencil above the line involved. If more space is needed, use the margins. Put a caret ($_\wedge$) at the exact place in the text where an interpolation is to be made. If necessary for clarity, draw a line leading from the caret to the passage you wish inserted.

Lengthy insertions may require the use of extra sheets. For example: a lengthy insertion is desired on page 1. Put a caret at the exact place, and put "Insert A" in the margin. On an extra sheet identified as page "1a" put "Copy A" and type the material needed. Subsequent insertions should be lettered consecutively as "Insert B" / "Copy B" (and so on). Any extra sheet should be made to follow the page on which the insertion is to be made, as: pages 2, 3, 3a, 4, 5, 5a. If more than one extra sheet is needed (3, 3a, 3b), this is a sign of poor organization, and the report should be redrafted.

The following correction symbols will save space in calling attention to desired alterations:

SYMBOL IN THE MARGIN	MEANING
ℐ	Delete that which has been crossed out or bracketed in pencil.
∧	[Caret]: insert marginal addition.
stet	Let it stand; material crossed out should be put back in.
ital	Italicize (underline) the words here underlined in pencil
caps	Capitalize letters or words double-underlined in pencil.

lc	Use lower case (small letters) where capitals have been crossed out with a slanting pencil stroke.
( )	Put parentheses where they are here penciled in.
[ ]	Put brackets where they are here penciled in.
	Note: some readers will put brackets around a passage in your text merely to define its exact limits, with instructions in the margin as to what is suggested—delete, substitute another wording, etc.
¶	Start a new paragraph.
no ¶	Do not begin a new paragraph, but "run in" as a continuation of the preceding paragraph.
#	Leave proper space.
⊐	Faulty alignment: move to the right.
⊏	Faulty alignment: move to the left.
⌒	Less space.
⌣	Close up entirely; no space.
∾	Transpose letters (words) into proper order. Or, if words to be transposed are widely separated, a penciled 1, 2, 3 above the words indicates the proper order.
⫲⫲	Short marks through an underscore: do not underline!
ⓘ	Query to author.
sp	Correct the spelling.
ⓢⓟ	Abbreviations or numerals should be spelled out.

Note the following marginal signs for inserting punctuation marks:

⋀	comma	⋀	semicolon
⋎	apostrophe	⊙	colon
⋓	quotation mark	⊙	period
-/	hyphen	?/	interrogation point
--/	dash		

8   Final draft

Where the report, term paper, or thesis is to be typed by the author, it is possible to proceed from any of the drafts previously described directly to the final typescript. But where the final typing

9

is to be entrusted to a professional typist, there should be a version identifiable as a "final draft" representing as closely as possible an *exact model* of what is to appear in the finished typescript. Typists are not mind readers; occasionally a whole thesis has had to be retyped because an author's intentions were not clear. Any written-in corrections should now be gone over in ink, for legibility. The neater the final draft, the fewer will be the typist's distractions, and hence the greater probability of a perfect typescript. This optimistic remark does not in the least obviate the *absolute necessity* of proofreading the finished typescript. Typists, being human, have been known to err.

9 The typescript

The remainder of Part One is devoted to all the various aspects of the typescript. Any preceding drafts that are "fair copy" should obviously follow the same rules. But as regards the finished, permanent typescript a final word may be said at this point: (1) in reports and term papers, a few last-minute corrections or insertions *in ink* are tolerated; but (2) in theses such inked-in corrections *may* or *may not* be tolerated, depending upon local regulations, regarding which one must inquire of the proper authorities.

II

THE TYPESCRIPT

10   The appearance of the page

In general, the typescript should be clean and neat, without ugly erasures, smears, stains, or creases. Damaged or disorderly pages should be typed over. Spelling, grammar, and punctuation should be correct and consistent. When in doubt, consult a dictionary for spelling, and a handbook of English composition for grammar. (See Bibliography.) Most of the relevant rules of punctuation are given below. Always read over the completed typescript to see that there are no inadvertent errors.

The *imperfect* typescript distracts the reader beyond all proportion; he will involuntarily dwell upon the imperfections, not giving full attention to what you have to say. The *perfect* typescript, on the other hand, miraculously melts into the background; the reader no longer notices the mechanics (and may not even praise you for them!), but can devote his concentrated attention to the content.

11   Paper

Type on one side only of good, white paper 8½ x 11 inches in size. Consider making a carbon copy of the report or term paper for your own files, in case the original should get mislaid.

For theses, library regulations usually prescribe the quality and weight of paper, as well as the number of copies to be furnished. Quality is usually stated in terms of rag content, as 100 per cent rag (the best), ranging downward to 50 per cent rag (the minimum for permanence without deterioration). "Weight" or "substance" is specified in terms of weight in pounds per ream of standard sheets before they are cut to usable sizes. Substance 20 (twenty-pound stock) is the standard weight, though substance 16, or even somewhat lighter papers are sometimes used, especially where several carbons are required. But never use onionskin paper, which is the ultimate in insults to any reader!

12 Typing

The typescript should be typed with double spacing throughout, except that matter which in a printed book would normally appear in reduced type should be single spaced, and centered headings are set off with triple spacing. (See rule 14.)

Some typewriters are equipped with vertical half spacing, which is a great convenience in typing superscript numerals. Owners of such machines quickly discover that they can get more on a page with one-and-a-half-spaced text. But this is analogous to printing a book in a smaller size type. When the novelty has worn off, it is best in the long run to return to standard double spacing.

The type should be clean, and the typewriter ribbon reasonably fresh. Experiment with type cleaners, which may be had at any stationery store, and use frequently. Keep a spare ribbon in your desk, so that when one gives out it can be quickly replaced.

13 Type faces

In the printing of a book or periodical, the typesetter has at his disposal:

Roman type in the size selected for the main body of the text, including CAPITALS, SMALL CAPITALS, and lower-case letters.

Italic type in the same size, *CAPITALS* and *lower case.*

Both roman and italic type in a smaller size for footnotes, or for matter such as long direct quotations to be inserted in the text.

Display type in larger sizes for headings.

Possibly other type faces for emphasis, such as **boldface.**

The typist, on the other hand, has only one kind and size of type at his disposal. By convention:

`lower case` letters are simply the ordinary small letters of the typewriter; first letters of words are capitalized where this is appropriate.

Italics are represented by underlining.

CAPITALS are used for display headings, such as the main title or chapter titles.

ITALIC CAPITALS are used almost solely for foreign words, or for titles, that appear within your own display headings, as:

THE CHORUSES OF HANDEL'S MESSIAH

Note, however, that when you cite such a title in your text, footnotes, or bibliography, the form is adapted as follows:
if a book title: The Choruses of Handel's "Messiah"
if a periodical article: "The Choruses of Handel's Messiah"

14 Spacing

In a general way, the spacing in the typescript serves as a substitute for the different sizes of type available to the printer.

Double space the main body of the text throughout.

Single space matter that would be set in smaller type in a book, as footnotes, long direct quotations, and the like.

Triple space display headings and centered captions. That is, leave three spaces below a main title or by-line. Leave three spaces above and below a centered heading inserted in the text.

SINGLE SPACING	DOUBLE SPACING	TRIPLE SPACING
Most typewriters	Leave a line	Leave two lines
will produce six		
lines of typing	vacant between	
to the inch,		vacant between
measured ver-	lines of typing	
tically up and		
down the page.		lines of typing.

15 Triple spacing

Leave three spaces: between a title or by-line and the beginning of the text (rule 27); before and after centered headings (rule 29); between two paragraphs where there is a decided break in thought. Do not use a row of asterisks to indicate a break in thought. If the break is important enough, put a centered heading.

16 Marks of punctuation and other signs

,	comma	**´**		acute accent
;	semicolon	**`**		grave accent
:	colon	**^**		circumflex accent
.	period	**ç**		c with cedilla (French, Portuguese)
–	hyphen			
——	dash (two hyphens)	**ñ**		n with tilde (Spanish)
?	question mark	**ã**	**õ**	vowels with til (Portuguese)
!	exclamation			
" "	quotation marks	**. . .**		ellipses (three spaced periods)
' '	single quotation marks			underline (underscore)
*	asterisk	**1 2 3**		Arabic numerals
&	ampersand	**I II**		Roman numerals
/	slant line (virgule)	**i ii**		small Roman numerals
( )	parentheses	**1**		superscript (above the line)
[ ]	brackets			
¨	English diaeresis; German umlaut; French tréma	**1**		subscript (below the line)
		. . .		leaders (used only in tables)

Signs not on the typewriter must be neatly hand-printed in ink. The most common typewriter keyboard is primarily for commercial use. In purchasing a machine, specify a "library" keyboard to obtain the brackets and foreign-language accents. Or consult your typewriter dealer regarding possible substitution of signs you expect to use frequently to replace signs seldom used.

17 Margins

Generous margins not only improve the appearance of the page, but also allow room to write comments or revisions. Recommended: Left margin, 1½ inches. Top, bottom, and right margins, 1 inch.

a. Left and right margins. First determine whether the type-

14

writer has pica or elite type by measuring a sample line. For pica type (10 letters to the inch), set left margin stop at 15 on the scale, right margin stop at 75. For elite type (12 letters to the inch), set left margin stop at 18, right margin stop at 90. Be sure that the left edge of the paper is fed into the machine at 0. (Cf. rule 31 Centering.)

Make a habit of leaving a generous left margin. If you later store your reports in a staple or clasp binder, up to ¾ inch of the left margin will disappear into the binding. Where full pages of musical examples are inserted into a report, it is a common fault to forget the left margin.

The right margin may be somewhat more flexible. The 1-inch recommendation is generous, and permits you to release the margin stop and type two or three letters beyond. Thus, a short final syllable of a word can be typed on the same line, without hyphenating. In formal papers, one should never type closer than ¾ inch from the right edge of the paper. In informal papers in pica type, this rule might perhaps be reduced to ⅝ inch. Inexperienced typists tend to be "margin shy" when starting a new page. Make a pencil mark at 75 (pica) or 90 (elite) as a guide to the space available for the first line of typing.

A right margin in perfect alignment (as in books) is called a "justified" margin. In typing, it is obviously impractical to attempt to justify the right margin. But avoid a grossly "ragged" margin, which is distracting to the reader.

b. Top margin. Use the variable spacer to align the top of the paper with the line scale. (The variable spacer is the button at the end of the cylinder for permanently changing the position of a line. The line scale is the straight-edge coinciding with the bottom of a line of type.) Center the page at 45 (pica) or 54 (elite). Drop down four spaces and put the page number on center. Drop down two more spaces and begin the first line of typing. This procedure leaves ½ inch (adequate) in the clear above the page number, and about 1 inch in the clear above the top line of typing.

If the page begins with a centered heading (rule 29), drop three spaces below the page number. For special treatment of the main title, see rule 26; for chapter headings, rule 159.

c. Bottom margin, without footnotes. Before inserting the paper in the typewriter, draw a penciled line in the left margin one inch from the bottom of the paper. When this line turns up, in the course of typing the page, you will know that you have reached the bottom margin. Another method: as your typing approaches the bottom of the page, measure (with a foot rule) the distance from the line scale to the top of the paper. It should be ten inches from the top edge of the paper to the beginning of the bottom margin.

d. Bottom margin, with footnotes. The main body of the text is double spaced, whereas the footnotes are single spaced. It is therefore rarely possible to have bottom margins on successive pages exactly the same. The margin may vary between 1 inch and ¾ inch.

Type the footnotes completely and accurately in the preliminary draft (rule 78). You will then know how many lines to allow for footnotes in the final typescript. Make up a "footnote guide" on a card and keep it near your typewriter. Such a guide should allow for the bottom margin and, beginning with line "1" at the margin, show a typed single-spaced column of numerals reading from the bottom upward: 1, 2, 3, 4, etc.

Before inserting the paper into the typewriter, calculate how many lines to leave for footnotes on that page. Add to the total *three additional lines* (i.e., the space between the last double-spaced line of text and the first footnote), and put a penciled mark in the margin. As you type, when this line turns up it is time to leave off the main text and begin the footnotes.

18 Paragraph indention

Indent the first line of each new paragraph five spaces.

19 Recessed left margin for single-spaced matter

Type with single spacing such matter as would normally appear, in a book, in reduced type: long direct quotations (rule 172), including poetry (rule 131a), or other extended verbal matter introduced by way of illustration (rule 131). Recess the left margin two spaces; that is, the single-spaced matter will have a new margin two spaces wider than the normal margin. Allow an addi-

TITLES, HEADINGS, CAPTIONS, LEGENDS

For reports and term papers, it is recommended that no title page be used. Put the main title and byline on the first page of text, with "sinkage" (i.e., extra space at the top of the page), as here described. For theses, see Section XIII.

26 Main title

Align the top of the paper with the line scale. Drop four double spaces. (For formal papers: two inches, i.e., six double spaces.) Put the main title, centered (rule 31), ALL IN CAPITALS and without terminal punctuation. Long titles may be laid out in two or more *double-spaced* lines, preferably of unequal length, with each line centered.

Never underline your main title for emphasis. However, foreign words or titles of published works appearing within your title should be underlined (italicized). See rule 13.

a. Subtitle. Where the main title includes a subtitle (optional), this should be introduced with a colon, as:

TWELVE-TONE TECHNIQUES IN STRAVINSKY:

AN ANALYSIS OF AGON AND THRENI

27 By-line

The by-line (centered) follows the main title and indicates authorship, as: By William Jones (i.e., your name, without terminal punctuation). Leave a *triple space* between main title and by-line, and between by-line and first line of text.

28 Book review

The recommended principal heading (main title) is simply BOOK REVIEW, with the by-line. Drop a triple space below the by-line and begin the book description, which is essentially like a *modified* bibliography entry (rule 113). Note the following differences: (a) author's name in normal order, first name first; (b) type double spaced; (c) all lines flush with left margin; (d) to suggest the qualities of a heading, type short lines of four or five inches instead of the normal six inches. Drop a triple space below the book description and begin your review, with normal paragraph indention. At the end of the review, drop a triple space below the last line and type your name flush with the *right* margin.

29 Section headings

Use centered headings to mark important divisions in the report, term paper, or thesis chapter. See rule 31 Centering. Put centered headings in lower case (small letters) with all important words (nouns, pronouns, adjectives, adverbs, verbs, first words) capitalized, and without terminal punctuation. Headings consisting of two or more lines should be double spaced. Leave a triple space above and below a centered heading.

Avoid putting a centered heading immediately below a main title or chapter heading. Plan one or more paragraphs of introductory material before the appearance of the first section heading.

Note: Headings are separate from the text, and not a part of it. Therefore, your text must be completely self-explanatory in itself, and not "lean" upon the headings. Learn to paraphrase, in order to avoid awkward repetition in the text of the exact wording of a heading.

30 Sideheads

A "sidehead" is typically a section heading that begins flush with the left margin. These are often used in printed books, but are not recommended for typescripts.

31 Centering

Main titles, chapter headings, section headings, and page numbers should be centered on the page. Because of the unequal left and right margins, *page center* is not the same as the center of the paper. Page center is 45 on the line scale for pica type, 54 for elite type. Some elite machines are 11-pitch (eleven characters per inch) rather than 12-pitch.

TYPE	LEFT MARGIN STOP	CENTER	RIGHT MARGIN STOP
10-pitch pica	15	45	75
11-pitch elite	16	49	82
12-pitch elite	18	54	90

To center a short title, place the carriage at "center," then backspace once for each two letters (or spaces) in the title.

For a long title, count the total number of letters and spaces in the line of title; subtract one half of the total from "center," and set the carriage immediately at the resulting number. Example (12-pitch elite): The title comprises a total of 40 letters and spaces. Half of 40 is 20. Subtract 20 from 54 (center). The result is 34. Set the carriage at 34 on the scale and begin the title.

32 Captions

A caption is a brief explanatory heading or remark placed immediately *above* a musical example (rule 132) or a table (rule 135). Depending upon the amount of emphasis desired, a caption may be: (a) all in lower case (small letters), with the first word and proper nouns capitalized; (b) in lower case, with all important words capitalized; or (c) as a display heading for an elaborate table, ALL IN CAPITALS. A caption consisting of two or more lines should be single spaced.

33 Legends

A legend is a title or other descriptive matter placed *below* a figure (rule 133) or a plate (rule 134). A legend is usually in lower case with only the first word and proper nouns capitalized. But if the legend consists of a title *and* descriptive matter, the title may be ALL IN CAPITALS and the descriptive matter in lower case. A legend consisting of two or more lines should be single spaced.

IV

PUNCTUATION

The main purpose of punctuation is clarity. The finer points of punctuation are a matter of personal preference. But where your meaning is not clear to the reader, be prepared to forego personal preference in favor of clarity of expression.

34 Sentence construction

Effective punctuation depends upon an understanding of how sentences are constructed. Short, simple sentences that contain little more than a subject and predicate may require only a period at the end. But longer sentences that include modifying phrases and clauses require some attention to internal punctuation. For a discussion of sentence building, see rules 189-95.

Regarding modifying phrases, see rules 35 Comma and 194 Phrases. Main clauses of a compound sentence (rule 191) are separated by a semicolon (rule 36), unless the clauses are unusually brief (rule 35). For modifying dependent clauses, see rules 35 Comma and 193 Subordinate clauses.

35 Comma

It is "comma sense" to put a comma whenever a slight pause in reading the sentence aloud would assist the clarity of thought.

a. Put a comma before *and, but, for, or, nor, yet* when these conjunctions join independent clauses. However, if the clauses are very short, the comma may be omitted; if the clauses are very long, and internally punctuated with commas, a semicolon may be required.

b. Nonrestrictive modifiers (i.e., phrases or clauses that could be omitted without changing the meaning of the word modified) should be set off with commas. But restrictive modifiers (i.e., phrases or clauses that change the meaning of the word modified) should be written without commas.

c. Appositives and parenthetical remarks should be set off by commas. If a decided break is intended, use parentheses or dashes.

d. Where a long subordinate clause, or even a long phrase, precedes or follows the main clause, use a comma for separation.

e. In enumerating a series of three or more items, put a comma after each item, and also before the *and* or the *or* that precedes the last item.

f. Where several adjectives precede and modify the same noun, put a comma after each one except the last (i.e., do not separate the last adjective from its noun).

36   Semicolon

The semicolon can be very useful for bringing together independent clauses into a single sentence. This may improve sentence rhythm by eliminating awkward full stops (periods).

a. The clause following a semicolon must always contain a verb. (But a colon or dash may be followed by a group of words without a verb.)

b. A conjunctive adverb (rule 191b), preceded by a semicolon and followed by a comma, often helps to point up the relationship of two main clauses.

c. Put a semicolon between contact clauses (rule 191).

d. Put a semicolon before a coordinating conjunction (rule 191a) joining two main clauses if the clauses are long and involved.

e. Use semicolons to separate items in a series if the items themselves require internal punctuation with commas.

f. Where a series of items is formally introduced with a colon, separate the items with semicolons.

37   Colon

The colon may be used to call attention to what follows: (a) a

quotation or an example; (b) a series of items; or (c) an epigrammatic summation of ideas. Never use a dash with a colon (:--).

38   Period

Periods, of course, should be put at the ends of sentences. If
you use a period, be sure that your sentence is complete, with a
subject and a verb. Leave two spaces after a period before beginning the next sentence. A footnote must end with a period; a common fault is to omit the period when the footnote ends with a page
number. *Omit* the period: after centered titles and section headings; after page numbers in the top margin; after the footnote
numeral which begins a footnote; after any numeral enclosed in
parentheses.

39   Hyphen

In hyphenating words at the right margin, use correct syllabi-
fication; consult a dictionary if necessary. The margin recommended in rule 17a is generous enough to permit running two or
three letters into the margin to complete a word. Other uses of the
hyphen:

a. To join two words, the second of which is a noun, to produce
a compound word modifying that noun, as: fourteenth-century
manuscript; two-four time; a first-rate violinist; the key of E-flat
major.

b. To join compound numbers between twenty-one and ninety-
nine.

c. With certain prefixes and suffixes, especially where ambiguity
or awkward letter combinations would otherwise appear, as: pre-
existing; self-appointed; bell-like.

d. In French style, to join given names and place names, as:
Jacques-François-Fromental-Élie Halévy; Boulogne-sur-Mer; rue
Notre-Dame-des-Victoires.

As for compound words: two words commonly associated (e.g.,
folk song) may first acquire a hyphen (folk-song), and later become
one word (folksong). The status of any particular compound will
vary according to accepted usage as well as the individual style of
the author. Consult a good dictionary. Be consistent in the form
used throughout each piece of writing.

40 Dash

Since there is no dash on the typewriter, use two hyphens close together. The dash is normally used to separate a parenthetical remark or an aside from the rest of the sentence. Such an aside does not have to contain a finite verb. The dash should be closed up tight with the words it separates. Example: `Many of these sonatas--twenty, to be exact--contain fewer than four movements.  Opus 111 ends with a slow movement--a theme and variations.`

The dash can be very useful at times; but its overuse becomes an unpleasant mannerism. Learn to use comma, parentheses, and colon effectively.

41 Parentheses

Parentheses can be very useful. Without actually breaking the flow of one's discourse, they momentarily suspend it to permit the writer to convey supplementary information (comments, explanations, passing references) at the precise moment when it is needed. This "precise moment" may be within a sentence, or it may be between sentences.

The parenthesis "left" or "open" sign should never be preceded or followed by any other punctuation. The parenthesis "right" or "closed' sign may be followed by a comma (if the sense requires it), or by a period (as here). (But if your parenthetical remark—which, by the way, need not be a complete sentence—comes between sentences, then begin with a capital and end with a period *inside*.) Suggestions:

a. For a parenthetical remark, or aside to the reader, you have a choice of parentheses or dash (rule 40).

b. For an explanation (even a single word, such as a synonym or translation), parentheses are preferable.

c. A foreign title, or a foreign-language passage, may be immediately followed by an English translation in parentheses if this seems appropriate.

d. A passing reference for the reader's orientation may be put in parentheses if the formality of a footnote citation appears too cumbersome.

e. Other conventional uses of parentheses are mentioned elsewhere, as for the imprint (place: publisher, date) in a footnote citation.

f. Numbers (or letters) in parentheses may be used to establish clarity in enumerating a series of items, as: (a) where the items are complex and perhaps internally punctuated; or (b) where the reader has been led to expect an exact number of items, and will be grateful if you count them as you go along.

42   Brackets

If there are no square brackets [ ] on your typewriter, insert them by hand in these cases: (a) to enclose your interpolations in quoted matter—rule 175; (b) to supply missing data, especially in bibliographic references; (c) for an unavoidable parenthesis within a parenthesis.

43   Quotation marks

Where quotation marks are called for, American usage requires double quotation marks " " with the single exception noted below. Avoid the British usage of enclosing quotations in single quotation marks ' .'

a. Use quotation marks to enclose direct quotations run on as part of your text. Cf. rule 177 Opening a quotation.

b. Omit quotation marks from single-spaced quotations separated from the text. Cf. rule 172 Spacing.

c. For a quotation within a quotation, use single quotation marks.

d. A comma or period always goes inside quotation marks; a colon or semicolon goes outside, thus:

```
"comma,"   "period."   "colon":   "semicolon";
```

e. A query (?) or exclamation (!) goes inside quotation marks if actually in the original being quoted. But if you yourself are supplying the query or exclamation, put it outside.

f. Titles of articles, short poems, and the like, are enclosed in quotation marks (rule 126 Titles).

g. It is rarely necessary to use quotation marks and underlining simultaneously in typescript. If you quote a passage that is consistently in a foreign language, quotation marks suffice, and no underlining is necessary.

44 Apostrophe

Proper names of one syllable always take *'s* to form the possessive: Bach's, Brahms's, Schütz's, Fux's, Strauss's. Proper names of more than one syllable ending in *s* or *z* add the apostrophe only: Lassus', Perotinus', Berlioz', several composers' works.

Use *'s* for plurals of single letters and numerals: e's and o's; 1's, 2's, 12's, 20's. (But: ones, twos, twelves, twenties.)

Contractions should in general be avoided, but if you use them don't forget the apostrophe that shows where letters have been omitted: isn't, haven't, o'er (over), it's (it is). The possessive pronoun *its* does not take an apostrophe.

45 Underlining

Underline (italicize):

a. Titles of books and musical compositions mentioned in your text, footnotes, and bibliography. (But see also rule 126 Titles.)

b. Foreign words appearing in an English context. (But see also rule 64 Foreign words.)

In general, avoid underlining merely for emphasis. But if you are sure that your underlined material would be appropriate if set in italics in a book or article, then go ahead!

Do not underline your own main title, chapter headings, centered section headings, captions or legends. However, foreign words or titles of books and compositions appearing *within* such headings should be underlined.

46 Words discussed

To direct attention to a term being discussed, underline (italicize) the term when it first appears in the discussion. The rule applies to both English and foreign terms, neither of which need be underlined more than once during any particular discussion.

To direct attention to a nontechnical English word or expression, enclose it in quotation marks, as: The verb "to be" can often be replaced by a stronger verb. But where a series of such terms would be embarrassing because of the accumulation of quotation marks ("of," "by," and "at" are prepositions), underlining may be substituted (of, by, and at are prepositions).

Capitalizing common nouns merely for emphasis is old-fashioned style, to be avoided.

47   Slant line (virgule)

This mark / is used:

a. When two or more lines of quoted poetry are run into your text (rule 131a).

b. When a lengthy title is given with bibliographic accuracy and it is desired to indicate the various lines in the original (rule 131b).

48   Ellipsis

The sign of ellipsis . . . consisting of three spaced periods is used to indicate the omission of material from a direct quotation. Cf. rule 176.

V

NUMERALS, DATES

49 Numerals

The three types of numerals available are:

Arabic	1	2	3	4	5	6	7	8	9	10
Roman	I	II	III	IV	V	VI	VII	VIII	IX	X
Small Roman	i	ii	iii	iv	v	vi	vii	viii	ix	x

To type Arabic numeral one, use small "1" and never capital "I"; if there is no zero on the typewriter, use capital "O" and never small "o."

Remember the peculiarities of Roman numerals: XL (40), L (50), XC (90), C (100), CC (200), D (500), M (1000), MDCCLXII (1762), MCMVII (1907).

50 Numbers in your text

In general, a number used incidentally in the text to express a total is spelled out if it is less than a hundred, or a round number. Always spell out a number that begins a sentence. Hyphenate compound numbers between twenty-one and ninety-nine, and most fractions: two-thirds, one and one-half.

If more than two or three words would be needed, use numerals: 326; 1256 or 1,256; 55½.

For numbers designating an individual item, a good rule is to use a numeral *after* the item, but spell out the number *before* the item: page 1, the first page; measure 23, the twenty-third measure; volume II, the second volume.

51   Arabic numerals

Use Arabic numerals for musical examples (rule 132), figures (rule 133), and page numbers in your typescript (rule 22) except for preliminary matter (rule 52).

52   Roman numerals

Use large Roman numerals for volumes, parts, chapters, tables, plates, and individuals in a series (Henry VIII). However, where higher numbers are involved, consider using Arabic numerals throughout: plates I-CXLIX, or plates 1-149.

Use small Roman numerals for preliminary pages (rule 153).

Use large and small Roman numerals, respectively, for acts and scenes of a play: Act I, scene ii; or *Julius Caesar, I, ii.*

53   Inclusive numbers

It is usually simplest to give both numbers in full: pp. 21-28, 345-346.

Alternatively, the following rules may be used. (a) Repeat tens: 11-15, 17-19. (b) But if the next to the last figure in the first number is a cipher, do not repeat this: 107-9. (c) Do not repeat hundreds or thousands: 345-46, 1213-57; British Museum Add. 12867-68, 30488-90, 10120-215. (d) But if the first number ends in two ciphers, give both numbers in full: 1800-1803.

54   Dates

The usual style for dates is "June 12, 1966," or "June, 1966," with a comma both before and after the year. (Naturally, at the end of a sentence the second comma would be replaced by a period.) Alternatively, an adaptation of French style might be: "12 June 1966" or "June 1966" without the commas. Whichever style is used must be maintained consistently.

Note: "the 1890's" but "the nineties."

Avoid abbreviations such as "7-6-1922" or "7/6/22" for "July 6, 1922." Note that German-style abbreviation reverses the date and month, as "6. VII. 1922" for "6 July 1922."

55   Inclusive years

The simplest style is to give both years in full: 1776-1791; 1803-

1809; 1900-1907. This is a necessity for years before the Christian era, which represent a diminishing series: 460-429 B.C.

Alternatively, the following rules may be used. (a) Within the same century, give only the last two figures for the second date: 1554-55; 1601-75; 1776-91. (b) But do not repeat a cipher as next-to-the-last figure: 1801-2; 1902-9; 1903-27. (c) If the century changes, or if the first date ends in two ciphers, write out both years in full: 850-1450; 1500-1600; 1770-1827; 1899-1900; 1800-1801; 1900-1966.

Note: One can put "from 1951 to 1955" or "during 1951-55" or "he lived 1756-1791" or even "from the period 1951-55" (considering that range of years as a point of departure). But never use the expression "from 1951-55" with both "from" and the hyphen.

Where the inclusive dates are more complete, use the dash instead of the hyphen: June 12, 1944—May 25, 1945; December 1965 —March 1966.

56 Centuries

References to centuries may be spelled out or abbreviated: "eighteenth century" or "18th century." Be consistent in your own usage, but (a) when presenting a direct quotation, follow the original exactly; and (b) in footnotes, you may abbreviate to save space, except in titles cited, which must be exactly like the original.

Hyphenate when "century" is part of a compound modifier (rule 39): "eighteenth-century forms" or "18th-century forms"; "17th- and 18th-century opera."

Note the Italian designations for centuries: *trecento*—1300's (14th century); *quattrocento*—1400's (15th century); *cinquecento* —1500's (16th century); *seicento*—1600's (17th century).

VI

SPELLING, FOREIGN WORDS,

ABBREVIATIONS

57 Spelling

Spelling should be correct and consistent in accordance with accepted American usage. Make a habit of using a dictionary. If you have serious trouble with spelling, obtain one of the many writers' manuals that contain lists of commonly misspelled words.

58 Musical terms

An occasional lapse in the spelling of an unusual or even common English word is excusable, but the misspelling of musical terms is *inexcusable*. In your reading, pay attention to spelling (but see rule 59). Many musical terms are found in standard general dictionaries, as well as in specialized music dictionaries.

Attention is called to the following Italian terms, so commonly used in English as to require no underlining, but frequently misspelled by students:

a cappella	obbligato
accelerando	pizzicato
appoggiatura	staccato
dilettante	toccata

59 American versus British usage

In our research, many sources of information—beginning with the ubiquitous *Grove's Dictionary*—will be by British authors who follow British usage. American usage differs from British usage in certain details. Samples of American spelling [British version in brackets]:

behavior, honor, humor, labor, rigor   [-our]
center, meter, theater   [-tre]
program   [-mme]

However, if you are citing a title or giving a direct quotation, spell as in the original.

60 Verbs in -ise or -ize

A common problem is to decide whether a verb ends in *-ise* or *-ize*. Consult a dictionary. The following brief list is suggestive:

-ise	advertise	exercise
	advise	improvise
	arise	revise
	disguise	supervise

-ize	analyze	italicize
	authorize	organize
	characterize	realize
	civilize	recognize
	criticize	summarize
	harmonize	symbolize

Note that verbs in *-ize* tend to have corresponding nouns ending in *-ization*. But analyze, analysis [*never* analyzation!]; criticize, criticism; summarize, summary.

61 Adjectives in -ible or -able

Most such words end in *-able*, so that the problem is to remember which ones end in *-ible*, as:

accessible   sensible
intelligible   visible
responsible

Words ending in *-e* usually drop the *-e* when adding *-able*:

sale, salable   use, usable

But -*ce* or -*ge* at the end is retained:

change, changeable	notice, noticeable
manage, manageable	peace, peaceable

62   Special plurals

Some words adopted from foreign languages retain their original plurals, as:

crisis, crises	genus, genera
criterion, criteria	thesis, theses
datum, data	stratum, strata

Others have acquired alternative English plurals, as:
appendix; appendices or appendixes
index; indices or indexes
focus; foci or focuses
formula; formulae or formulas
beau; beaux or beaus
cherub; cherubim or cherubs (-*im* is a Hebrew plural)
seraph; seraphim or seraphs

63   Miscellaneous words

The following spellings are recommended. Where dictionaries give alternate spellings, the implication is that the first version presented is preferable.

acknowledgment	gaiety
adviser	goodbye
aesthetic	gray
cannot	judgment
catalogue	labeled
descendant (noun)	medieval
enroll	practice (noun and verb)
focused	principal (foremost)
forego	principle (fundamental truth
farther (in spatial distance)	or rule of action)
further (in time, quantity or	rhyme
degree)	rhythm

35

foreword (preface)   skillful
forward (onward)   technique
fulfill   toward

64   Foreign words in English context

Underline (italicize) foreign words appearing in an English context. However, foreign words that have been absorbed into almost daily English speech need not be underlined, as for example: alma mater, apropos, bona fide, bourgeoisie, café, chef d'oeuvre, dilettante, dramatis personae, ersatz, et cetera, ex officio, façade, genre, hors d'oeuvres, laissez faire, matador, naïveté, nom de plume, status quo, Weltanschauung.

Among musical terms, Italian words were generally among the first to become embedded in the English language, as: aria, cantata, capriccio, concerto, crescendo, fantasia, gamba, intermezzo, maestro, opera, sonata, verismo.

From the French we have: allemande, amateur, ballade, chanson, clavecin, courante, fauxbourdon, nocturne, and so on.

German terms are less readily absorbed, partly because of the embarrassing German habit of capitalizing common nouns, though words like gebrauchsmusik, ländler, leitmotiv, lied, minnesinger, etc., are sometimes freely used in lower case.

There remains, however, the possibility of underlining for emphasis (rule 45), or because particular words are being discussed (rule 46), or even for the more subtle purpose of bringing out the foreign flavor of the words. Use good judgment, and avoid cluttering up the page with *too many* underlined words.

One can generally put up with more italicized words in print than are endurable in typescript. It is recommended that the usual practice of underlining be discontinued for: circa (ca.), et al., fl., ibid., loc. cit., op. cit., q.v., sic, s.v. In any case *do not* underline the Latin abbreviations: cf., e.g., etc., viz., vs.

But underline words which, in rapid reading, might not otherwise be quickly understood, as: *infra, passim, supra, vide.*

In preparing copy for the printer, be guided by the recommendations of your editor.

65   Foreign quotations

If you present a passage that is entirely in a foreign language, either in quotation marks in your main text or set off with single spacing, no underlining is necessary. But underline the occasional word within such a context that may be foreign to that language, as: "c'était un vrai *gentleman*"; "zu dieser Zeit war es *comme il faut*."

66   Accents and diacritics

An "accent" mark, properly speaking, would show stress. "Diacritical" marks represent a broader category of signs that may be attached to either vowels or consonants to indicate a particular sound that differs from the sound of the unmarked letter. Copy all such marks faithfully.

German. The umlaut (¨) with ä, ö, ü changes the pronunciation of the vowel, and often the meaning of the word.

French. The acute (´), grave (`), and circumflex (^) accents are used with vowels: été, là, père, fête. The *tréma* (¨) indicates separate pronunciation of a second vowel: Noël; naïf, Saül. The cedilla (¸) softens c: façade, façon, reçu.

Italian. The grave accent (`) shows stress: città, perchè, però, più.

Spanish. The acute accent (´) shows stress: catálogo, lírico, canción, música. The tilde (˜) softens n: mañana, español.

Portuguese. The accents (´ ` ^) indicate vowel shadings. The *til* (˜) over a and o indicates slight nasalization: São, põe. The cedilla (¸) softens c: canção, março.

Czech. The diacritics over vowels do not indicate stress, but lengthen the vowel (á, ě, í, ó, ú, ů, ý) without much change of quality. The hook (*haček*) over a consonant changes the sound: č = *ch*; ň like Spanish ñ; ř = *rzh*; š = *sh*; t̛ as in hi*t y*ou; ž = *zh*.

Polish. Vowels a and e are nasalized with the subscript hook (ą, ę); ó as in m*oo*n; diacritics over consonants change the sound [ć = *ch*; ń = *ñ*; ś = *sh*; ź and ż are variants of *zh*]; ł is pronounced back in the throat, almost like *w*.

Hungarian. Accents indicate not stress, but length of vowel; the stress is always on the first syllable of the word. Greatly simplified, it could be said that the short vowels are a, e, i, o, ö, u, ü, and the long vowels á, é, í, ó, ő, ú, ű.

Scandinavian. Vowels ä and ö are pronounced approximately as in German. Swedish also has å (= o), while Danish and Norwegian have ø (= ö).

In transliterations of other languages (e.g., Middle Eastern, Asiatic) one may find the *macron* over vowels (ā, ē, ī, ō, ū); the subscript dot under consonants (d̩, h̩, s̩, t̩, z̩); and possibly still other signs, such as the breathings in Greek and Arabic.

67 Spelling of foreign words

In German all nouns are capitalized. Some foreign languages inflect the articles *the* and *a, an* according to gender and number:

German—der, die, das, des, dem, den; ein, eine, eines, einem, einen.

French—le, la, l', les; un, une.

Italian—il, la, lo, l', gli, gl', le; un, una, uno, un'. ˙

Spanish—el, la, los, las; un, una.

Portuguese—o, a, os, as; um, uma.

Polish, Czech, and Russian have masculine, feminine, and neuter genders but do not use any articles, either definite or indefinite.

Hungarian—definite article: a, az (before vowels); indefinite: egy (which also means "one").

Swedish—definite article is added at the end of the word: -en, -n, -et, -t, -na, -a, -ena; indefinite article precedes the word: en, ett.

Danish and Norwegian—definite article (suffixed): -en, -n, -et, -t, -ne, -ene; indefinite (precedes): en, et.

Dutch—de, het, 't; een.

As a rule (to which there are individual exceptions), French and Italian names do not capitalize the separated particles *le, la, de, du, di, da,* etc., when these are preceded by a given name or title: Josquin des Prez; Vincent d'Indy; Pierre de la Rue; Lorenzo da Ponte; le chevalier des Grieux; Count di Luna. The particle is capitalized when part of a last name standing alone: Des Prez;

D'Indy; La Rue; Da Ponte; Des Grieux; Di Luna. Unseparated particles are always capitalized as part of the name: Debussy; Deslandes; Dubois; Lavigna; Lesueur. Note that French given names in series are usually hyphenated: Achille-Claude Debussy; Charles-Louis-Ambroise Thomas.

Certain letters and letter combinations may seem less arbitrary if their approximate pronunciation in the original language is kept in mind. Key: *ch* (*church*); *ts* (ha*ts*); *sh* (*sh*oe); *zh* (azure).

German—tsch (*ch*); sch (*sh*).

French—ch (*sh*); j (*zh*).

Polish—cz, ć (*ch*); c (*ts*); sz, ś (*sh*); ź, ż, rz (*zh*); szcz (*shch* as in ca*sh ch*eck).

Czech—č(*ch*); c (*ts*); š (*sh*); ž (*zh*).

Hungarian—cs (*ch*); c, cz, tz (*ts*); s (*sh*); zs (*zh*); sz (sharp *s* as in Liszt).

Distinguish carefully the spelling of foreign words that are similar to English words. Examples:

ENGLISH	GERMAN	FRENCH	ITALIAN	SPANISH
music	Musik	musique	musica	música
symphony	Symphonie	symphonie	sinfonia (*-ee'-ah*)	sinfonía
sonata	Sonate	sonate	sonata	sonata
fantasy	Phantasie (or F-)	fantaisie	fantasia (*-ee'-ah*)	fantasía
quartet	Quartett	quatuor	quartetto	cuarteto
rhythm	Rhythmus	rythme	ritmo	ritmo
correspond- ence	[Brief- wechsel]	correspond- ance	[carteg- gio]	correspon- dencia
democracy	Demokratie	démocratie	democrazia (*-ee'-ah*)	democracia
bassoon	[Fagott]	basson	[fagotto]	bajón
dance	Tanz	danse	danza	danza

68   Checklist of days, months, cities, countries

In foreign-language quotations beware of misspelling a word because it is similar to English, or to some other foreign language

with which you may be more familiar. The following checklist may
serve to illustrate some of the pitfalls.

ENGLISH	GERMAN	FRENCH	ITALIAN	SPANISH
Monday	Montag	lundi	lunedì	lunes
Tuesday	Dienstag	mardi	martedì	martes
Wednesday	Mittwoch	mercredi	mercoledì	miércoles
Thursday	Donnerstag	jeudi	giovedì	jueves
Friday	Freitag	vendredi	venerdì	viernes
Saturday	Samstag (Sonnabend)	samedi	sabato	sábado
Sunday	Sonntag	dimanche	domenica	domingo
January	Januar (Jänner)	janvier	gennaio	enero
February	Februar	février	febbraio	febrero
March	März	mars	marzo	marzo
April	April	avril	aprile	abril
May	Mai	mai	maggio	mayo
June	Juni	juin	giugno	junio
July	Juli	juillet	luglio	julio
August	August	août	agosto	augusto
September	September	septembre	settembre	septiembre
October	Oktober	octobre	ottobre	octubre
November	November	novembre	novembre	noviembre
December	Dezember	décembre	dicembre	diciembre
Antwerp	Antwerpen	Anvers	Anversa	Amberes
Florence	Florenz	Florence	Firenze	Florencia
Geneva	Genf	Genève	Ginevra	Ginebra
Milan	Mailand	Milan	Milano	Milán
Munich	München	Munich	Monaco	Munich
Naples	Neapel	Naples	Napoli	Nápoles
Venice	Venedig	Venise	Venezia	Venecia

Note also the following special forms:
Aix-la-Chapelle—Aachen (Ger.)
Brussels—Bruxelles (Fr.)
Cologne—Köln (Ger.)
Leipzig—Lipsia (It.)
London—Londres (Fr., Sp.), Londra (It.)

Paris—Parigi (It.), París (Sp.)
Prague—Prag (Ger.) Praga (It., Sp.), Praha (Cz.)
Rome—Roma (It.)
Vienna—Wien (Ger.), Viena (Sp.)

England	England	Angleterre	Inghilterra	Inglaterra
Germany	Deutschland	Allemagne	Alemagna	Alemania
Hungary	Ungarn	Hongrie	Ungheria	Hungría
Italy	Italien	Italie	Italia	Italia
Poland	Polen	Pologne	Pologna	Polonia
Scotland	Schottland	Écosse	Scozia	Escocia
Spain	Spanien	Espagne	Espagna	España
Switzerland	Schweiz	Suisse	Svizzera	Suiza
United States	Vereinigte Staaten	États-Unis	Stati Uniti	Estados Unidos

Note also the special forms:
Austria—Österreich, Oesterreich (Ger.), Autriche (Fr.)
France—Frankreich (Ger.), Francia (It., Sp.)

69   Transliteration of Russian

Russian employs the Cyrillic alphabet, and there are different systems for transliterating into the Roman alphabet. The practice employed by the Library of Congress is widely used by librarians, and is recommended for very accurate transcription from Russian-language sources.

Many names and titles of works first made their way into English usage via German or French transliterations, as: Tschaikowsky, Scriabine. Adaptation to American usage has been gradual and not always consistent, as: Tchaikovsky; Scriabin or Skriabin; Prokofiev or Prokofieff.

On p. 42 will be found the Cyrillic alphabet, in capital and lower-case letters. (Where no capital is given the letter cannot occur at the beginning of a word.) Column 3 shows the LC transliterations.

While the Library of Congress system is always *correct*, one may prefer to follow common usage for well-known names and titles. Suggested simplifications of the LC system are here given in brackets.

А	а	a		Ф	ф	f	
Б	б	b		Х	х	kh	
В	в	v		Ц	ц	t͡s	[ts]
Г	г	g		Ч	ч	ch	
Д	д	d		Ш	ш	sh	
Е	е	e		Щ	щ	shch	
Ё	ё	ë	[e]		ъ	″	*hard sign* [omit]
Ж	ж	zh			ы	y	
З	з	z			ь	′	*soft sign* [omit]
И	и	i		Э	э	ė	[e]
	й	ĭ	[i]	Ю	ю	i͡u	[yu *or* iu]
К	к	k		Я	я	i͡a	[ya *or* ia]
Л	л	l		*old forms:*			
М	м	m		I	i	ī	[i]
Н	н	n		Ѣ	ѣ	i͡e	[e]
О	о	o		Ѳ	θ	ḟ	[f]
П	п	p		V	v	ẏ	[y]
Р	р	r		*endings:*			
С	с	s			ий	iĭ	
Т	т	t			ая	ai͡a	[aya]
У	у	u			ыи	yĭ	[y]

The following names may be compared in Cyrillic, LC, and modified spellings:

Балакирев	Balakirev	
Бородин	Borodin	
Глинка	Glinka	
Даргомыжский	Dargomyzhskiĭ	Dargomyzhsky
Кащей	Kashcheĭ	Kashchei
Кюи	Ki͡ui	Cui
Мусоргский	Musorgskiĭ	Musorgsky
Прокофьев	Prokof'ev	Prokofiev
Рахманинов	Rakhmaninov	
Римский—Корсаков	Rimskiĭ-Korsakov	Rimsky-Korsakov
Советская Музыка	Sovetskai͡a Muzyka	Sovetskaya Muzyka
Царь	T͡sar'	Tsar
Юрий Шапорин	I͡Uriĭ Shaporin	Yuri Shaporin

Cyrillic spellings of familiar non-Russian words, names, and titles may be disregarded as:

Бах	Bach
Бетховен	Beethoven
Брамс	Brahms
Шопен	Chopin

Note special spellings of Koussevitzky (or Koussewitzky), and such Polish names as Stokowski, Landowska, Leschetizky.

70   English and Latin abbreviations

(See also 71 German and French abbreviations.) The following common abbreviations are frequently met with in scholarly writing, and may be freely used wherever abbreviations are in good taste, particularly in citations and parenthetical references. Capitalize where appropriate, as at the beginning of a footnote, or where matter immediately preceding is closed with a period.

Abbreviations here *italicized* should be underlined in typescript. Italics in the explanatory column merely indicate Latin derivation; such terms and their abbreviations *may* be underlined in typescript if this seems essential for clarity.

Note carefully whether the abbreviation or term *is* or *is not* followed by a period. Quotation marks here used enclose a definition or call attention to a word or phrase, and are *not* to appear in the typescript.

anon.	anonymous
ante	"before"; previously mentioned
arr.	arranged, -ment
art., arts.	article(s)
b.	born
bibliog.	bibliography, -er, -ical
biog.	biography, -er, -ical
bk., bks.	book(s)
c	copyright; without period or space, to show copyright date, as: c1928 (rule 92)
c., ca.	*circa*, "about"; used with approximate dates, as: ca. 1400. The form "ca." is preferable
cf.	*confer*, 'compare"; do not use "cf." where "see" is intended

Ch., Chs., Chap., Chaps.	Chapter(s)
col., cols.	column(s)
comp.	composer, -ed, -ition
d.	died
diss.	dissertation
ed., eds.	editor(s), edition(s); after a title, "ed." may stand for "edited by"
ed. cit.	*editione citata,* "in the edition cited"
edn., edns.	edition(s); may be used instead of "ed., eds." to avoid confusion with "editor(s)"
e.g.	*exempli gratia,* "for example"; preceded and followed by punctuation: , e.g., or ; e.g.,
enl.	enlarged, as in "rev. enl. ed." (revised and enlarged edition)
esp.	especially, as in "meas. 19-35, esp. 26"
et al.	*et alii, aliae, alia,* "and others"
et seq.	*et sequens,* "and the following" (see "f., ff.")
etc.	*et cetera,* "and so forth"
ex., exx.	example(s)
f., ff.	used after a numeral to mean "and the following page (f.) or pages (ff.)"
fac., facsim.	facsimile
fasc.	fascicle
fig., figs.	figure(s)
fl.	*floruit,* "flourished, reached greatest development of influence"
fn.	footnote (see "n.")
fol., fols.	folio(s)
front.	frontispiece (an illustrative plate that precedes the title page in a book)
hist.	history, -ical, -ian
ibid.	*ibidem,* "in the same reference" (rule 99)
idem	(without period), "by the same author" (rule 99)
i.e.	*id est,* "that is"; preceded and followed by punctuation: , i.e., or ; i.e.,
illus.	illustrated, -ion(s)

infra	"below"; later in the discussion (see *supra*)
intro., introd.	introduction
l., ll.	line(s), as in "p. 6, l. 17 and ll. 23-25"—not generally recommended because of confusion with Arabic "1" (one)
loc. cit.	*loco citato*, "in the place cited" (rule 99)
meas.	measure(s)
MS, MSS	(without period), manuscript(s); however, British publications favor "Ms., Mss."
n., nn.	note(s); commonly used instead of "fn" (see rules 78, 80)
N.B.	*nota bene*, "note well"
n.d.	no date; used where no publication date is given, as "London: Novello, n.d." (rule 113d)
No., Nos.	number(s), usually capitalized; avoid #
n.p.	no place; used (rarely) to indicate that no place of publication is given (rule 113c)
N.S.	New Series, New Style (cf. O.S.)
numb.	numbered
op. cit.	*opere citato*, "in the reference cited" (rule 99)
Op., Opp.	Opus, Opera, "work(s)"; capitalized before the number of a specific work, as "Op. 106"
O.S.	Old Style; used principally to indicate dates not in conformity with the Gregorian calendar
p., pp.	page(s); omit if volume number precedes, as "II, 356"; the plural form is used only preceding a group of inclusive pages, as "pp. 15-20"
par., pars.	paragraph(s)
passim	"throughout the work, here and there"; used where it would be tedious to give all the page references where a given thing is mentioned or discussed
per cent	(two words, without period)
pf.	pianoforte
pl., pls.	plate(s); capitalize when referring to specific plates, as "Pl. XVI" (note the possible confusion with "place")
post	"after, later"; not recommended unless in a mean-

45

	ingful Latin phrase, as: *post diem* (after the set, or proper, day); *post hoc* (after this)
pref.	preface; and *avoid* abbreviating "preferably"
pseud.	pseudonym, *nom de plume* (pen name), fictitious name
Pt., Pts.	Part(s); used to refer to subdivisions that are so designated, as "Pt. III"
publ.	published, published by, publication(s)
pubs.	publications; inelegant, better avoided
q.v.	*quod vide,* "which see"; normally follows a term which the reader is expected to look up under that heading; may be put in parentheses or italicized: "Sonata" (q.v.) or "Sonata," *q.v.*
r	*recto,* "right-hand page"; written superscribed without period after a folio number, as "fol. 27^r" (see *verso*)
recte	"correctly, properly"; used to signal true name or proper spelling
rectius	"more correctly, more properly"
reg.	registered
rev.	revised
sc.	scene, as "sc. ii"; not recommended—better: "I, ii" (Act I, scene ii), or "scene ii"
Ser.	Series; used to designate a particular series, as "Ser. II"
seriatim	"in a series"; as adverb (or adjective)
st.	stanza; not recommended—cf. "street" and "Saint"
St., SS.	Saint(s); used preceding the name, as "St. Louis, St. Paul's Cathedral, SS. Peter and Paul" (cf. rule 71, "St, Ste")
supra	"above"; earlier in the discussion (see *infra*)
s.v.	*sub voce, sub verbo,* "under the heading or word"; precedes a term which the reader may find under that heading, as: *Harvard Dictionary of Music,* s.v. "Sonata"
transcr.	transcribed, -iption; after a title, "transcr." may stand for "transcribed by"

trans., tr.	translated, -or, -ion; after a title, may stand for "translated by"
v	*verso*, "reverse, or left-hand page"; written super-scribed without period after a folio number to indicate the reverse side of that folio, as "fol. 27ᵛ" (see *recto*)
vcl.	violoncello
vla.	viola
vln., vl.	violin
vide	"see"; followed by a reference which the reader may look up (see also "q.v.")
viz.	*videlicet*, "namely" (the *z* is a corruption of medieval Latin *-et*); appropriate for conveying the meaning "that is to say"; requires punctuation: , viz., or , viz.:
vol., vols.	volume(s); capitalize when followed by a numeral (Vol. I); lower case when preceded by a number (2 vols.); omitted when followed by a page reference (II, 356)
vs. .	*versus*, "against"; loosely: "compared with"

71 German and French abbreviations

The following list will serve to acquaint the student with some of the more common abbreviations encountered in German and French scholarly writings.

a.a.O.	am angeführten Ort, "in the reference cited"; like "op. cit."
Anh.	Anhang, "appendix"
Anm.	Anmerkung, "note"; like "n., fn."
Aufl.	Auflage, "edition"
Ausg.	Ausgabe, "edition"
Bd., Bde.	Band, Bände, "volume(s)"
Bearb.	Bearbeiter, -ung, "editor, version"; lower case *bearbeitet von*, "edited by"
Begl.	Begleitung, "accompaniment"
bzw.	beziehungsweise, "or, respectively"
c.-à.-d.	c'est-à-dire, "that is"; like "i.e."

Cie	Compagnie, "company"
das.	daselbst, "in the same place"; like "loc. cit."
dgl.	der-, desgleichen, "similarly"; u. dgl., und desgleichen
ebenda	"in the same place"; like "ibid."
evang.	evangelisch, "Protestant" or specifically "Lutheran"
evtl.	eventuell, "perhaps, possibly"
fr.	francs (monetary unit)
geb.	geboren, "born"
gest.	gestorben, "died"
gen.	genannt, "mentioned, surnamed"
G.m.b.H.	Gesellschaft mit beschränkter Haftung, "limited (liability) company"; loosely equivalent to "Co., Ltd."
h.	heure, "hour"; 10 h., "10 o'clock"
Hs., Hss.	Handschrift(en), "manuscript(s)"
hrsg.	herausgegeben, "edited"
Jh., Jahrh., Jhdt.	Jahrhundert, "century"
K., Kap.	Kapitel, "chapter"
k.k.	kaiserlich-königlich, "imperial-royal" (Austria)
kais.	kaiserlich, "imperial"
kath.	katholisch, "Catholic"
kgl.	königlich, "royal"
kl.	klein(e), "small"
Lbd.	Leinband, "cloth binding"
M.	Monsieur, "Mr.": plural: MM. (Messieurs, Mssrs.)
Mlle	(without period) Mademoiselle, "Miss"; plural: Mlles
Mme	(without period) Madame, "Mrs."; plural: Mmes
ms., mss.	manuscrit(s), "manuscript(s)"
né, née	"born" (masc., fem.)
N.-D.	Notre-Dame, "Our Lady"
N^o, n^o	numéro, "number"; like "No."

Nr.	Nummer, "number"; like "No."
o.J.	ohne Jahr, "without year"; like "n.d."
ouvr. cit.	ouvrage cité, "in the reference cited"; like "op. cit."
resp.	respektiv, "respectively"; often with the force of "and, on the other hand"
S.	Seite, "page"; like "p."
s.	siehe, "see"
s.a.	siehe auch, "see also"
S.A.	Son Altesse "His (Her) Highness"; S.A.R., Son Altesse Royale
S.M.	Sa Majesté, "His (Her) Majesty"
sog.	sogenannt, "so-called"
St, Ste	(without period) Saint(e), "Saint" (masc., fem.)
s.v.p.	s'il vous plaît, "if you please"
t.	tome, "volume"
u.	und, "and"
u.a.	unter andern, "among others"; und andere, "and others"
übers.	übersetzt, "translated"
u.s.w.	und so weiter, "and so forth"
v.	von, vom, "by, from, of"
verb.	verbessert, "revised, improved"
Verf.	Verfasser, "author"
verm.	vermehrt, "enlarged, increased"; vermählt, "married"
vgl.	vergleiche, "compare"; like "cf."
Vᵉ	veuve, "widow"
voir	"see"
z.B.	zum Beispiel, "for example"
z.Z.	zur Zeit, "at the time, at present, acting (president, etc.)"

Numerals, Dates

1ᵉʳ, 1ᵉʳᵉ	premier, première, "first"
2ᵉ, 2ᵐᵉ	deuxième, "second"
XVᵉ siècle	quinzième siècle, "15th century"

den 1.	den ersten, "the first"
im XIX. Jh.	im neunzehnten Jahrhundert, "in the 19th century"
6. VII. 1922	"6 July 1922"
7bre	septembre, "September"
Xbre	décembre, "December"

VII

FOOTNOTE REFERENCES

72 Footnote logic

Footnotes are used mainly for two purposes: (a) to refer the reader to sources of information—rules 72-99; and (b) to provide explanatory comments, or additional evidence, which would interrupt the main flow of ideas if incorporated into the text—rules 100-105. In writing for the general public, footnotes may be kept to a minimum, or avoided entirely. But for the scholarly report, term paper, or thesis assume that your readers will be both knowledgeable and critical, and will constantly ask: *Where did you get this particular information? Who says that the facts are thus? Whose opinion are you stating?* The purpose of footnote documentation is to anticipate such queries. One must learn to judge where citations are expected, and where they may be safely omitted.

73 Documentation of facts

Facts may be loosely grouped into three realms: (a) *Common knowledge*—things that are readily accessible in most standard reference works, and hence generally known to anyone at all conversant with the subject. (b) *Special knowledge*—things mentioned by only one or a few persons, such as specialists or experts, and hence not generally known. (c) *Personal knowledge*—things which the writer-investigator has observed for himself, which may agree with, or supplement, or even repudiate the findings of common knowledge and special knowledge. Statements of fact from the realm of common knowledge are usually not documented. (Exception: beginners who want practice in footnoting may be rather liberal with documentation.) Statements of fact from someone else's fund of special knowledge must always be duly credited and documented. Statements of fact from the writer's own personal knowledge are usually incorporated into the body of the paper. Where such statements seem to supplement (or repudiate) what is already known, it is wise to explain where and how the observation was made.

Remember that if you do not give a citation it is assumed that your statement of fact is either (a) common knowledge, or else (b) your own personal observation, for which you assume full responsibility.

74   Documentation of opinion

An opinion is what someone thinks or believes about something. There may be differences of opinion even regarding the nature of facts, as in the well-known story of the three blind men and the elephant. In general, though, an opinion is a point of view which someone has arrived at after reviewing and assessing factual information and drawing inferences and conclusions. Observe the rules of property: (a) some opinions are in the public domain; (b) some are clearly the private property of individuals; (c) some may be your own personal property.

An opinion that is stated without documentation is assumed to belong to the writer whose by-line appears at the head of the report. Where you have taken the trouble to formulate an opinion, your very manner of presenting the facts and arguments should make this sufficiently clear. Or you may merely share an opinion that is widely held, not particularly controversial, or so logical as to seem obvious, in which case no documentation need be given.

Where you borrow an opinion that clearly belongs to another, by all means credit the source. Then, if it turns out to be a bad opinion, you will already have attached the blame to its original author. If a good opinion, you and your source mutually substantiate each other, and you are in good company.

75   When to give credit

A commonly held misconception is that only direct quotations require documentation. Actually, statements of fact and opinion are far more often brought into a discussion in the form of abstract or paraphrase (rules 170, 171), where the logic of documentation is still fully applicable.

76   Footnote numbers in the text

In double-spaced matter, footnote numbers are typed as super-scripts ("superior numbers") a half space above the line. Put the number, without leaving a space, immediately after the word in the text. If the word is followed by punctuation, the superscript is placed after the punctuation.

In single-spaced matter, numbers typed as superscripts will run into the line above. In the interests of neatness, one might avoid footnoting until the end of the single-spaced matter, then leave a space and type the number on the line. (Cf. rule 77.)

The footnote number is usually placed at the *end* of a connected statement or quotation requiring documentation. But if the citation applies only to a single term, or only to a portion of a statement, the superscript must be carefully placed to reflect accurately which information was obtained where.

It is a usual courtesy to mention an author's name before presenting what he has to say in abstract, paraphrase, or direct quotation. If the wait would be too long between the name and the end of the statement, attach the footnote immediately to the author's name.

Two or more superscripts occurring together are separated by commas. But see rule 86 Plural references.

Footnotes should be numbered consecutively throughout the report, paper, or chapter. (In theses, begin a new series of footnote numbers for each new chapter.) Regarding the problem of renumbering when footnotes are added or deleted, see rule 78.

77   Form of the footnote

Wherever footnote superscripts appear in the text, the eye should be able to drop to the bottom of the *same page* and find there the footnotes, typed with single spacing analogous to reduced type (rule 14).

Regarding space allowance for footnotes, see rule 17d.

After completing the last line of main text for which there is room on the page, drop a *single space*. Using the underscore key (never the hyphen), begin at the left margin (flush) and type a continuous line fifteen spaces in length. To keep such "footlines" (or "rules") uniform throughout the typescript, a memorized rhythmic pattern will help:

(If a longer line is desired, add another triplet.)

Drop another two spaces, and you have reached the level of the first footnote.

For each footnote: Indent *two spaces* from the left margin, type the footnote number *on the line* (without punctuation), leave *two spaces* after the number, and begin the footnote. Adequate trial should convince the typist that this is the neatest form. Over-generous indention wastes space. Typed superscript numerals are messy. (The printer's superscripts are special small figures that never ascend higher than the tallest letters in the line.) By avoiding superscripts, it becomes unnecessary to leave space between footnotes.

After the first line of a footnote (indented as above), run any subsequent lines of the same footnote out to the left margin. "Hanging" indention, as used in the bibliography, is not appropriate in footnotes.

If a footnote is too long to fit on the same page, it may be continued on the next page, separated from the main text by the usual footline. Plan the continuation so that the reader is forced to turn the page to complete the sense. Or put (continued) flush with the right margin.

End each footnote with a period. A common fault is to neglect to put a period after a page number concluding a footnote.

78   Footnotes in a draft

In the preliminary drafts of a paper, it is a great convenience to put in the notes immediately, as needed, without waiting for the bottom of the page. Type a line, flush with the left margin, both *before* and *after* the note to separate it from the main text. Such notes should be complete and in proper form; it then becomes a simple matter to transfer them to the bottom of the page in the final typescript. (Cf. rule 17d.)

The problem of *renumbering* footnotes often arises, because of additions or deletions made in the process of revision. The form here recommended for the draft has the advantage that no numbers are needed: a superscript *n* (for "note") suffices, since the note is immediately at hand. When preparing the fully revised draft for final typing, go through and number the footnotes consecutively in proper order.

In desperation, to avoid complete renumbering of a long sequence of footnotes, insertions such as 1, 1a, 2, 2a, 2b, 3 might do.

79 Footnote style

We speak of footnote "sentences" which are not actually complete sentences, but which are internally punctuated according to certain conventions and end with a period. Observe carefully the models given, and see also rules 100-105.

Any footnote citation should give, as completely and accurately as possible, yet in the tersest possible form, all the information needed *at that particular point*. When a source of information is first cited in a paper, or in a chapter of a thesis, follow the' rule for *First Reference*. Subsequent citations of a source that has already been thus fully described should follow the rule for *Short Reference*.

80 Books

a. First reference. Give author's full name, in normal order, *comma*, book title, underlined [no comma], publication information in parentheses (Place, *colon*: Publisher, *comma*, date), *comma*, page reference, *period*. The page reference usually indicates one particular page[1] where information was found. But if the statement or discussion cited involves more than one page, give the inclusive pages.[2,3] Avoid the use of "pp. 112f" [p. 112, and the following page] and "pp. 115ff [p. 115, and the following pages]. If the book title comprises more than one volume, give volume number as well as page.[4] To refer to a footnote on a given page, put "n" [for "note"] after the page number.[5] (Models on p. 56.)

1 Harold C. Schonberg, <u>The</u> <u>Great</u> <u>Pianists</u> (New York: Simon and Schuster, 1963), p. 221.

2 Gilbert Chase, <u>America's</u> <u>Music</u> <u>from</u> <u>the</u> <u>Pilgrims</u> <u>to</u> <u>the</u> <u>Present</u> (New York: McGraw-Hill, 1955), pp. 433-35.

3 F. T. Arnold, <u>The</u> <u>Art</u> <u>of</u> <u>Accompaniment</u> <u>from</u> <u>a</u> <u>Thorough-Bass</u> <u>as</u> <u>Practiced</u> <u>in</u> <u>the</u> <u>XVIIth</u> <u>and</u> <u>XVIIIth</u> <u>Centuries</u> (London: Oxford University Press, 1931), pp. 318-22.

4 . . . Vol. II, p. 561. Or better yet: . . . II, 561.

5 . . . p. 142n.

(Note: An ellipsis here means that, in these examples, the rest of the citation has been omitted to save space.)

There are times when a truly full description of the source would clutter up the footnote. Omit lengthy subtitles (cf. rule 113b). See rules 84-91 for possible complications. Include what is necessary for clear identification of the source, and leave the full description to the Bibliography (rule 113).

b. Short reference. (1) Give author's last name only, unless first names or initials are necessary to avoid confusion.[6] (2) Use only as much of the title as needed to make it sound literate and readily identifiable.[7] For complicated titles, resort to ellipsis.[8] (3) Omit place, publisher, date, and other information already given in the first reference, and proceed directly to the page reference.

6 Schonberg, <u>The Great Pianists</u>, p. 223.

7 Chase, <u>America's Music</u>, p. 439.

8 Arnold, <u>Art of Accompaniment</u> . . . , pp. 172-202.

81 Articles in periodicals

a. First reference. Give author's name, in normal order, *comma*, title of article, in quotation marks, *comma*, name of periodical, underlined, *comma*, volume number [no comma] year, in parentheses, *comma*, page reference, *period*. Where both volume and page are given, the abbreviations "Vol." and "p." are omitted.[9] Some writers prefer an Arabic numeral for the volume, in which case it must always be separated from the page number by a colon.[10] If a volume number is missing or irrelevant, give month and year,[11] or season and year,[12] or exact date of publication.[13] If authorship cannot be determined, begin with the title.[14] If there is not even a proper title, describe the item in your own words, without quotes.[15]

9   Guido Adler, "Style-Criticism," Musical Quarterly, XX (1943), 173.
10   . . . 65 (1887): 136-37.
11   Ronald Eyer, "Metropolitan Opera Introduces The Rake's Progress to America," Musical America, March 1953, p. 3.
12   Gunther Schuller, "Conversation with Varèse," Perspectives of New Music, Spring-Summer 1965, pp. 32-37.
13   Olin Downes, "Original Boris: Composer's Ideas to be Followed at the Met," New York Times, March 1, 1953, Section 2, p. 7.
14   "Professional Opportunities," Journal of Music Therapy, IV (1967), 76-78.
15   Specifications for a chapel organ at Sweet Briar College, Holtkamp advertisement in The American Organist, Vol. 49 (February 1966), p. 19.

b. Short reference. Give author's last name, and title of article; omit other information given in the first reference, and proceed directly to the page reference.[16] The title may be shortened,[17] using ellipsis if desired.[18]

16   Adler, "Style-Criticism," p. 174.
17   Downes, "Original Boris," p. 7.
18   Eyer, ". . . The Rake's Progress," p. 3.

82   Articles in dictionaries and encyclopedias

a. First reference. Signed articles should be attributed to the author whose name or initials are given, usually at the end of the article. (If initials only are given, take the trouble to find out the full name!) Treat much as you would a periodical article.[19] If the article is unsigned, you may attribute it to whoever is responsible for the whole publication.[20] Where the edition used is a factor (rule 91), this should be mentioned.[21] Where proper authorship seems immaterial, begin with the title.[22] The editor's name may also be useful.[23]

19 Hans F. Redlich, "Mahler," Die Musik in Geschichte und Gegenwart, VIII, 1490-99.

20 Willi Apel, "Chanson," Harvard Dictionary of Music, p. 129.

21 George Hipkins, "Harpsichord," in Grove's Dictionary of Music and Musicians (3rd ed., 1927), II, 545.

22 Article "Alois Hába," in Baker's Biographical Dictionary of Music and Musicians (5th ed., 1958), p. 633.

23 Article "Singing," in Grove's Dictionary of Music and Musicians (5th edn., edited by Eric Blom, 1954), VII, 803.

b. Short reference. Give as much as is necessary to make it clear that you are again referring to a source already cited.

24 Redlich, "Mahler," MGG, p. 1496.

25 Apel, "Chanson," Harvard Dictionary, p. 130.

26 Hipkins, "Harpsichord," Grove's, II, 546.

27 Baker's, "Alois Hába," p. 633.

28 Grove's, "Singing," VII, 804.

83 Sections in symposia, etc.

a. First reference. If it seems desirable to call attention to a chapter title in an author's book, treat as a combination of article and book.[29] Where several authors have contributed to a symposium, collection, or miscellany, identify the whole book as well as the individual essay.[30] If the citation becomes complicated, some of the information may be put in parentheses.[31]

29 Paul Henry Lang, "The Renaissance,"

Chapter 9 in <u>Music</u> <u>in</u> <u>Western</u> <u>Civilization</u> (New York: Norton, 1941), pp. 289-92.
30 Kathleen Dale, "The Piano Music," in <u>The</u> <u>Music</u> <u>of</u> <u>Schubert</u>, edited by Gerald Abraham (New York: Norton, 1947), p. 112.
31 Robert Haas, "Die Oper im 18. Jahrhundert," in <u>Handbuch</u> <u>der</u> <u>Musikgeschichte</u>, edited by Guido Adler (2nd ed.; Berlin: Max Hesse, 1930), II, 718.

b. Short reference. Enough should be given to make it clear that you are referring back to the same source already described.

32 Lang, "The Renaissance," in <u>MWC</u>, p. 291.
33 Dale, "The Piano Music," p. 113.
34 Haas, "Die Oper im 18. Jahrhundert," in Adler's <u>HMg</u>, II, 719.

84 Volume in a series

It is usually too cumbersome to include the series title in a footnote.[35] Such information belongs more properly in the bibliography (rule 113i). On rare occasions, one may wish to mention a volume subtitle.[36,37]

35 Walter H. Rubsamen, <u>Literary</u> <u>Sources</u> <u>of</u> <u>Secular</u> <u>Music</u> <u>in</u> <u>Italy</u> <u>(ca.</u> <u>1500)</u>, in University of California Publications in Music, Vol. I, No. 1 (Berkeley and Los Angeles: University of California Press, 1943), p. 59.
36 Léon Vallas, <u>Vincent</u> <u>d'Indy</u>, Vol. I: <u>La</u> <u>Jeunesse</u> (Paris: Albin Michel, 1946), p. 101.
37 Vallas, <u>Vincent</u> <u>d'Indy</u>, Vol. II: <u>La</u> <u>Maturité,</u> <u>La</u> <u>Vieillesse</u> (Paris: Albin Michel, 1950), pp. 134-35.

85 Reviews

a. First Reference. Reviews of books,[38] music,[39] and recordings[40] are useful sources of information and opinion. These citations are likely to be somewhat cumbersome at best.

38   Jan LaRue, review of Vincent Duckles,
Music Reference and Research Materials (New
York: Free Press of Glencoe, 1964), in Journal
of the American Musicological Society, XIX
(1966), 258.
39   Charles Hamm, review of Guillelmi Dufay,
Opera Omnia, Tomus VI (Cantiones), edited by
Heinrich Besseler (Rome: American Institute of
Musicology, 1964), in Musical Quarterly, LII
(1966), 252-54.
40   Paul Henry Lang, review of Handel's Serse
(recording, Westminster WST 321), in Musical
Quarterly, LII (1966), 396.

b. Short reference. If you have had occasion, in a previous footnote, to cite directly the work reviewed, then obviously even the first reference to the review can be shortened.[41] (Note that long titles of well-known periodicals may be abbreviated.) If the discussion in your text is skillfully handled, subsequent references to the same review can be quite short.[42]

41   Jan LaRue, review of Duckles, Music Reference and Research Materials, in JAMS, XIX
(1966), 258.
42   Hamm, review cited.

86   Plural references

If more than one reference is given in the same footnote sentence, separate the references with semicolons.[43] Such a plural reference eliminates the need for more than one reference number at the same place in the text.[43,44] In introducing the reader to a subject, it may be convenient to cumulate a selection of "required reading" in one footnote.[44]

43   David Cherniavsky, "The Use of Germ Mo-
tives by Sibelius," Music & Letters, XXIII
(1942), 8; Gerald Abraham, editor, The Music of
Sibelius (New York: Norton, 1947), pp. 35-36;
William G. Hill, "Some Aspects of Form in the

Symphonies of Sibelius," Music Review, X (1949),
182.

44   See Norman Demuth, "Alban Berg," Chapter
20 in Musical Trends in the Twentieth Century
(London: Rockliff, 1952), pp. 239-45; Paul
Collaer, "Arnold Schoenberg, Anton Webern, Alban
Berg," Chapter 2 in A History of Modern Music
(trans. by Sally Abeles; Cleveland: World Pub-
lishing Co., 1961), pp. 92-113; Peter S. Hansen,
"Berg and Webern," Chapter 9 in An Introduction
to Twentieth Century Music (Boston: Allyn and
Bacon, 1961), pp. 198-208.

87   Place: publisher, date

If it is necessary to save space in the first reference, give whichever is the more readily recognizable: *place* or *publisher*, followed
by a comma, and the date. But if the reference would otherwise be
obscure, give both.

Samples: . . . (London, 1853) . . . (Paris, 1905) . . . (Oxford
University Press, 1963) . . . (Prentice-Hall, 1965) . . . (Bärenreiter,
1965) . . . (Cambridge, Mass.: Mediaeval Academy of America,
1949) . . . (New York: Dover, 1965) . . . (Bari: Laterza, 1962) . . .
(Wiesbaden: Breitkopf & Härtel, 1962).

Omit *The, Inc., Ltd.*, etc., and *Co.* when not needed to complete
the sense, as Boston Music Co. First names or initials of publishers
may be omitted, unless necessary to avoid confusion, as E. C.
Schirmer [not G. Schirmer].

Regarding the validity of publication dates, see rule 91 Edition
used.

88   Joint authorship

Where two authors are jointly responsible for a work cited, give
both names.[45] If three or more authors, give only the name of the
first, followed by "and others" or "et al."[46,47]

a. First reference

45   Wallace Brockway and Herbert Weinstock,

Men of Music (New York: Simon and Schuster, 1939), p. 311.

46   Beekman C. Cannon and others, The Art of Music (New York: Crowell, 1960), p. 322.

47   Paul Collaer et al., Atlas historique de la musique (Paris: Elsevier, 1960), carte (map) 7, facing p. 40.

b. Short reference

48   Brockway and Weinstock, Men of Music, p. 312.

49   Cannon, Art of Music, p. 345.

50   Collaer, Atlas historique, p. 58.

89   Editor

Where a responsible author can be found for a work, put the author's name first, and "edited by" after the title.[51] But if original authorship is sufficiently clear in the title, begin with the title.[52] The editor of a miscellaneous collection may be mentioned first.[53] But see also rule 83 regarding the crediting of individual essays in collections.

a. First reference

51   Charles Burney, A General History of Music, edited by Frank Mercer (New York: Harcourt Brace, 1935), II, 16.

52   The Letters of Richard Wagner: The Burrell Collection, edited by John N. Burk (New York: Macmillan, 1950), p. 372.

53   Oliver Strunk, editor, Source Readings in Music History (Norton, 1950), p. 707.

b. Short reference

54   Burney, History, II, 25.

55   Burk, Letters of Richard Wagner, p. 376.

56   Strunk, Source Readings, p. 709.

90   Translator

Give the original author, with "translated by" after the title.[57,58]

a. First reference

57 Johann J. Quantz, On Playing the Flute,
trans. by Edward R. Reilly (New York: Free Press
of Glencoe, 1966), p. 46.
58 André Gédalge, Treatise on the Fugue,
trans. by Ferdinand Davis (University of Okla-
homa Press, 1965), pp. 284-95.

b. Short reference

59 Quantz, On Playing the Flute, p. 118.
60 Gédalge, Treatise on the Fugue, p. 170.

91 Edition used

Statements of fact or opinion may vary in different editions of
the same work. Identify the edition used, and verify the date at
which the particular passage cited appeared in print. A *reissue,
printing,* or *reprinting* (see rule 113g) may bear a later date on the
title page; check the verso of the title page for the date of the
edition—this is what carries weight in the timing of the author's
statement or comment. Examples:

61 Cecil Forsyth, Orchestration (2nd ed. ;
New York: Macmillan, 1935), p. 115.

Note: The copy consulted was "Reprinted, 1946." The statement
may have been made already in the first edition (1914). Forsyth
died in 1941, and it seems plausible that, in any case, he believed
in this statement as of 1935.

62 Hugo Riemann, Musik-Lexikon, 12th edn.
edited by Wilibald Gurlitt, Vol. I (Mainz: B.
Schott's Söhne, 1959), p. 336.

Note: Without exhaustive checking through various editions, one
cannot be sure who is responsible for any particular statement. At
least the *edition used* is adequately described.

63 Ernest Newman, The Life of Richard Wagner,
Vol. III (New York: Knopf, 1941), p. 266.
Note: It took Newman some thirteen years to bring out all four

volumes of his biography. The statement cited was in Vol. III, first issued by Knopf in 1941, even though the date of the second printing (1948) appears on the front of the title page.

92 Musical editions

When referring to a passage in a musical score, cite the edition used. Underline the title of the composition if it occupies the whole volume. [64,66] ("Volume" is here loosely used to mean whatever is contained between two covers, whether a few pages of sheet music or a complete opera.) But if there are several different compositions in the volume, put the title of the work in quotation marks, followed by the volume title underlined.[65,67] Since publication dates are seldom given for music, use the copyright date: c [without period] followed by the year, without space between.[65,66,67] Where relevant to the discussion, mention the editor.[66] If the volume used is part of a series, give the series title as well.[67]

64 Maurice Ravel, <u>Pavane</u> <u>pour</u> <u>une</u> <u>infante</u> <u>défunte</u> (Eschig edn., n.d.), p. 3.
65 Claude Debussy, "Le vent dans la plaine," in <u>Préludes</u>, 1er Livre (Paris: Durand, c1910), pp. 7-12.
66 Franz Liszt, <u>Sonata</u> <u>in</u> <u>B</u> <u>Minor</u>, ed. by Rafael Joseffy (G. Schirmer, c1909), p. 8.
67 Frédéric Chopin, "Nocturne," Op. 15, No. 2, in <u>Complete</u> <u>Works</u>, Vol. VII, <u>Nocturnes</u> <u>for</u> <u>Piano</u> (Warsaw: Chopin Institute, c1952), p. 39.

a. Measure numbers. The safest procedure is to count measures consecutively through an entire movement, beginning with "measure 1" as the first *complete* measure.[68] If the reader refers to a different edition he can still find the place. But where you are reasonably sure that the reader will use a readily available standard edition: (a) Perhaps measure numbers are already printed in the score.[69] (b) If not, give the page number and count as 1-2-3-etc. the measures appearing on that page.[70] (c) If there are several systems (or "scores"), put in parentheses: system, *colon:* measures.[71] (See also rule 128 regarding measure references in the text.)

68 Franz Schubert, "Der Wanderer," meas.
32-40.

69 Tchaikovsky, Symphony No. 6, in B minor
(Kalmus min. score), third movement, meas. 275-
78, 299-300.

70 Joseph Haydn, "Quartet," Op. 54, No. 3, in
Kalmus edn., 30 Celebrated String Quartets, Vol.
II, p. 5, meas. 10-14.

71 J. S. Bach, "Praeludium XIX," in The Well
Tempered Clavichord (Kalmus edn.) Vol. I, p.
86 (5: 2), p. 87 (1: 1-2).

93 Recordings

As a minimum, give the composer, title of composition, record
company, and issue number. As much more information may be
given as seems pertinent to the discussion. Examples:

72 Bartók, Concerto No. 3 for Piano (Vox
11490).

73 Mozart, Symphony No. 38 in D, "Prague,"
K. 504 (Beecham; Columbia ML-4313).

74 Prokofiev, Piano Concerto No. 3, recorded
by Byron Janis and the Moscow Philharmonic
Orchestra, Kyril Kondrashin conducting (Mercury
MG 50300).

75 Weber, "Euryanthe Overture," in A
Toscanini Omnibus, Arturo Toscanini and the NBC
Symphony Orchestra (RCA Victor LM-6026), side
2, band 2.

76 Webern, "Five Canons on Latin Texts," Op.
16, in Webern: The Complete Music (Columbia
K4L-232), side 4, band 2.

By analogy, for a field recording on tape, give as much as the
reader needs to know. Compare and adapt rule 118a.

a. Record jackets. Information may be gleaned from the jacket
(or "sleeve," or "liner") accompanying a record, or in the pamphlet
or brochure accompanying an album. If such material is signed,
give the commentator's name.

77   Bruno Walter, jacket notes for Mahler, Symphony No. 1 in D (Columbia ML 5794).

78   Thurston Dart, jacket notes for Orlando Gibbons: Tudor Church Music (Westminster XWN 18165).

79   Robert Craft, brochure for Webern: The Complete Music (Columbia K4L-232), p. 10.

94   Manuscripts

Reference to early manuscripts, composers' autographs, and the like, presupposes sufficient research experience for the student to make proper citation in accordance with conventional usage. If there is room for misunderstanding as to whether you are using the original or a photocopy, make this clear in your discussion of the source and in the bibliography (rule 117). Published facsimiles should be described as such.

95   Theses

Titles of master's theses and doctoral dissertations are usually put in quotation marks, without underlining. Mention the institution and date.

80   Shirley Munger, "Gigue Types in Keyboard Music from John Bull to J. S. Bach" (Master's thesis, University of Washington, 1950), p. 14.

81   Mary Jane Corry, "The Keyboard Music of Juan Cabanilles: A Stylistic Analysis of the Published Works" (Ph.D. dissertation, Stanford University, 1966), p. 64.

96   Letters

When citing published letters, make sure that (besides the usual reference to the published source) it is clear *who* was writing *to whom* on *what date*. This information may be given either in the body of your text, or in the footnote. Example: [Text] On 9 July 1778, Mozart wrote to his father[82] the sad news of his mother's death in Paris.

82   Emily Anderson, The Letters of Mozart and

His Family (2nd ed.; London: Macmillan, 1966),
II, 561.

Where you have elicited information from someone through
direct correspondence, give the date and identify the recipient as
"the present writer."[83]

83 Lloyd Hibberd, in a letter of September 7,
1964, to the present writer.

97   Iconographic materials

Sometimes, in your writing, you may mention or describe visual
objects that are artistic (paintings, sculpture, architecture) or
documentary (photographs, maps, drawings). Regarding the inclusion of figures and plates in your paper, see rules 133, 134. If
you do not include illustrations, refer the reader to a published
source where he can find a reproduction of the thing described.

84 Positive organ of the early 14th century,
in Frank Ll. Harrison, Music in Medieval Britain
(London: Routledge and Kegan Paul, 1958), Plate
XI, facing p. 140.

85 The Concert, painting by G. B. Panini
(Paris, Louvre), shows a performance of Leonardo
da Vinci's La contesa dei numi at the Polignac
palace, Rome, November 27, 1729. See Marc
Pincherle, An Illustrated History of Music,
trans. by Rollo Myers (New York: Reynal, 1959),
p. 123.

86 For the seating plan of the orchestra at
the Teatro San Carlo in Naples in 1786, see
Heinz Becker, "Orchester," Musik in Geschichte
und Gegenwart, X, 178, fig. 3.

87 For a photograph of Tin Pan Alley, ca.
1916-17, see Jablonski and Stewart, The Gershwin
Years (Garden City,N.Y.: Doubleday, 1958), p.
50. George Gershwin worked here at Remick's,
and his brother Ira worked next door for the
New York Clipper.

98 Interviews, etc.

Where information has been obtained orally, mention the name of your informant in the text and give the gist of what was said in abstract, paraphrase, or indirect discourse. You may use quotation marks only if you have taken the precaution to secure a *verbatim* statement. In a footnote, give the date and circumstances. Note that when you write down an oral statement you are providing permanent documentation for that statement. In the following examples, it is assumed that you have already given the informant's name and statement in your text.

```
88   In an interview of March 7, 1967.
89   In a public lecture on "Problems of
Criticism in Modern Music," Bradley Hall, West-
ern University, May 25, 1966.
90   In a lecture on Brahms, course in "Late
19th-Century Music," September 27, 1967.
91   In a conversation with the present writer
on November 7, 1966.
```

99 Op. cit., ibid., idem, loc. cit.

Caution: Many readers and editors object strongly to the use of these abbreviations, and insist upon a standard short reference (rules 80ff.). However, for closely documented passages where constant repetition of a title or author's name would be cumbersome or redundant, the abbreviations can be very convenient. Never force the reader to refer back more than three or four pages to discover the full meaning. If there have been many intervening footnotes, refresh the reader's memory with a standard short reference. In typescript style, where a paper is not being submitted for publication, these abbreviations need not be underlined.

Op. cit. (opere citato: "in the work [reference] cited") replaces a title only. [92,94] Give author's name and page reference.[94] If you have referred to more than one work by the same author,[93,95] obviously "op. cit." must be avoided as confusing.[98]

Ibid. (ibidem: "in the same place [reference]") refers to the author and title given in the footnote immediately preceding, and may be followed by a page reference.[95,96] When ibid. is *not* followed by a page reference, it refers to precisely the same page(s) as those given in the preceding footnote. In closely documented papers, ibid. may be used in series (analogous to ditto marks in a vertical column),[96,97] but any footnote[98] that refers to a different source breaks the chain.

Idem ("the same person [author]") is not an abbreviation, and must not be followed by a period. The word stands for the same author as in the footnote immediately preceding,[98] and is followed by a *different title* by that author and a page reference.[99]

Loc. cit. (loco citato: "in the place [passage] cited") should be avoided as too vague. The example here given[100] presumably (?) refers to Dart, op. cit., p. 73.

92 Thurston Dart, The Interpretation of Music (London: Hutchinson, 1954), pp. 31-33.

93 Robert Donington, The Instruments of Music (London: Methuen, 1949), pp. 80-86.

94 Dart, op. cit., p. 73.

95 Robert Donington, The Interpretation of Early Music (London: Faber and Faber, 1963), pp. 505-512.

96 Ibid., p. 510.

97 Ibid., p. 448.

98 Donington, Instruments . . . , p. 88.

99 Idem, Interpretation . . . , p. 300.

100 Dart, loc. cit.

VIII

FOOTNOTE DISCUSSION

100 Rationale

Besides serving the important function of documentation (cf. rules 72-74), footnotes may contain commentary or discussion that would otherwise interrupt the flow of ideas if incorporated into the main text of the paper or thesis.

101 Directives

An otherwise standard footnote citation may be introduced with one of the following directives:

See—implies that you have presented only the main gist of an extended argument or complex series of facts, and that the reader should consult the source cited for full details.[1]

See also—refers to still another source (besides any already mentioned) which corroborates your arguments or gives further details; implies that there is no room to deal with this additional item in the body of your text.[2]

But see—to refer to a source that differs with your own argument on minor or major points.[3] In order not to tease the reader, explain briefly the points of difference.

Compare—usually a challenge to the reader to look up the reference cited and compare it with your own argument.[4] *Compare* tends to suggest a blend of *see, see also,* and *but see.*

1 See Herbert Weinstock, <u>Handel</u> (2nd ed.; New York: Knopf, 1959), pp. 75-78.

2 See also William C. Smith, "The Earliest Editions of Handel's Water Music," Musical Quarterly, XXV (1939), 60-75.

3 But see Idem, Handel: A Descriptive Catalogue of the Early Editions (London: Cassell, 1960), pp. 255-60 and passim for updated information on editions.

4 Compare Newman Flower, George Frideric Handel (rev. ed. ; New York: Scribner's, 1948), pp. 122-25.

102 Running comment

The actual citation may be incorporated into a sentence of commentary.[5] The footnote sentence may be analogous to a compound sentence.[6] Or a footnote paragraph can be constructed, with more than one sentence.[7]

5 J. A. Westrup, "Monteverdi and the Orchestra," Music & Letters, XXI (1940), 230-45, has shown that the orchestra of Orfeo does not represent an innovation but is normal for the period.

6 "Edouard Commette," in Larousse de la musique, I, 214; according to the obituary in the Musical Times (July, 1967, p. 641), Commette died on April 21, 1967, at the age of eighty-four.

7 For more on Jean Barraqué (b. Paris, 1928), see André Hodeir, Since Debussy (New York: Grove Press, 1961), pp. 163-203. "Like Beethoven's greatest Sonatas," writes Hodeir, Barraqué's Piano Sonata is "conceived on a very large scale and lasts over half an hour."

103 Supplementary discussion, with citation

If you get involved with a side issue which has no place in the main text, consider dropping to a footnote to carry on such supplementary discussion. A citation may be given at the end of the footnote.[8]

8 The première of <u>Carmen</u> at the Opéra-
Comique was on 3 March 1875; it ran for fifty
nights during the 1875-76 season, and was not
revived until 21 April 1883. For an account of
problems at rehearsals, see Mina Curtiss, <u>Bizet</u>
<u>and His World</u> (New York: Knopf, 1958), pp.380-
86.

104 Parenthetical citation

Where a short reference will do, a convenient form is to put the
citation in parentheses at the end.[9]

9 The prelude to <u>Tristan</u> had been performed
at the Paris concert of January 25, 1860.
(Barzun, <u>Berlioz</u> <u>and</u> <u>His</u> <u>Century</u>, p. 355.)

105 Addenda

When the meeting is over, the discussion is continued in the
corridors! Any information, illustrations, polemics, and so on, that
cannot be gracefully incorporated into the main text may be carried
on in the footnotes—provided one does not abuse the privilege.

IX

BIBLIOGRAPHY

106 Placement

The bibliography always comes last, except that if an index is included it follows the bibliography. The Arabic page numbers of the typescript are continued consecutively through the bibliography (and also through the index, if present). For a long paper or thesis, begin the bibliography on a new page with the word BIBLIOGRAPHY in capitals, centered. For a shorter paper, where the main text occupies only part of the last page, by all means drop two double spaces below the end of the text, put BIBLIOGRAPHY centered, and use the space available.

107 Purpose

The bibliography serves an ethical function by notifying the reader as to the sources of the writer's information. It informs your reader (e.g., professor or critic) as to the materials and influences with which you have been in contact. If other students read your paper or thesis, and become interested in your subject, the bibliography provides them with a further course of study.

108 Items included

The following modifying terms should not be used in the heading. They are merely here explained as a guide to the logic of organization.

Selected bibliography—normally includes only such sources as were actually consulted, and which contributed directly or indirectly to the purpose of the study.

Complete bibliography—attempts to give an exhaustive list of the sources relevant to the subject. If items are included which *the writer has not seen,* this should be made clear in an explanatory note (rule 109) or in annotations (rule 112).

Unified bibliography—brings together all items, of whatever nature, into one general listing usually alphabetized by authors' or composers' last names.

Classified bibliography—arranges the sources into groups according to type or content, with a centered lower-case heading at the beginning of each classification. Examples:

Books and Articles	Original Sources	Literature
Music	Secondary Sources	Sources and Editions
Recordings		(A favorite classification with some German writers.)

Or, in the case of an extensive bibliography, any suitable grouping that promises to make the listing more usable and accessible.

Annotated bibliography—see rule 112.

109　Explanatory matter

Any special circumstances connected with the bibliography may be explained in a short single-spaced paragraph just below the centered heading. Typical matters requiring explanation: (a) symbols or abbreviations used in the entries; (b) unavailability of important sources not listed, or listed but not seen; (c) omission of obvious available sources; (d) general commentary on the whole bibliography, or on selected items therefrom.

110　Form

Use hanging indention. That is, begin the first line of each entry (e.g., author's name) flush with the left margin, and indent subsequent lines of the same entry four spaces. In typescript, the material is all single spaced, except that a blank space may be left between entries if desired.

111 Style

Whereas footnotes are laid out in "sentences," the bibliography is much more liberal with periods. See models in rules below, which are dogmatic only in the interests of consistency. Actually, styles vary widely, both as to layout and as to completeness and accuracy of content. The best models are found in published book reviews and book lists. Unfortunately, so-called bibliographies or checklists at the end of most books tend to be incomplete and ineffectual.

a. Numbering. Ordinarily, do not number bibliographic entries. For those rare instances where bracketed references in the text are approved for documentation, see rule 129.

b. Coded symbols. In scholarly writing that involves considerable documentation, footnote references are sometimes made more manageable by using standard coded symbols for books, periodicals, or music collections. Employment of such symbols (if approved) must be sophisticated and in accordance with the best practices in the published literature of the particular field. In any case, the symbols should be fully explained in the layout of the bibliography. For good models of how the system works, see the two books by Gustave Reese cited under rule 113a *Same author.*

112 Annotations

It is both good discipline and helpful to the reader to include an annotation (i.e., a brief comment on content or quality) for each bibliographic entry. Such a commentary may be: (a) directed toward the work as a whole, or (b) only toward those portions which are relevant; (c) in the writer's own words, or (d) an edited version of matter taken from the preface, chapter headings, etc., of the work being annotated.

```
Cooper, Martin.  French Music: From the Death of
    Berlioz to the Death of Fauré. London: Oxford
    University Press, 1951. 240 p.
    Discusses Fauré's early works, pp. 78-87, the
    middle period, pp. 140-43, and the late works,
```

pp. 211-14. See also the Table of Events 1870-
1925, pp. 220-34.

Einstein, Alfred. Schubert: A Musical Portrait.
New York: Oxford University Press, 1951. 343
p.
Arranged chronologically, but with emphasis
on Schubert's musical environment and inner
development rather than on the outward facts
of his life. A penetrating critical discussion.

Harrison, Frank Ll., Mantle Hood, and Claude V.
Palisca. Musicology. (The Princeton Studies:
Humanistic Scholarship in America.) Englewood
Cliffs, N.J.: Prentice-Hall, 1963. 337 p.
An important survey of the aims and methods
of musical scholarship. Harrison contributes
"American Musicology and the European Tradi-
tion," pp. 1-85; Palisca, "American Scholar-
ship in Western Music," pp. 87-213; Hood,
"Music, the Unknown" [ethnomusicology], pp.
215-326. For an illuminating commentary, see
Paul Henry Lang, "Editorial," Musical
Quarterly, 50 (1964): 215-26.

Haydon, Glen. Introduction to Musicology. New
York: Prentice-Hall, 1941. 329 p.
A survey of the fields, systematic and historical, of musical knowledge and research.
Chapters on acoustics, physiology and psy-
chology in relation to music, musical aes-
thetics, the theory of music theory, musical
pedagogy, comparative musicology. Pages 247-
99 devoted to philosophy, sources, problems,
and methods of music history. Basic bibliography for each subject covered, general
bibliography at the end.

Searle, Humphrey. "Ferencz Liszt," in Grove's
Dictionary of Music and Musicians. Fifth
edition, edited by Eric Blom. London: Mac-

```
millan; New York: St Martin's Press, 1954.
(Vol. V, pp. 256-316.)
Catalogue of works, pp. 263-316.
```

A. BOOKS

113   Books, standard entry

Always consult the title page, and also the reverse of the title page, for the information needed. In its simplest form, the entry should contain: author's last name, *comma*, given names, *period*. Full title, underlined, *period.*. Place, *colon*: publisher, *comma*, date, *period*. Number of pages, *period*. For various possible complications, see subheadings 113a-i below.

```
Bukofzer, Manfred F.  Music in the Baroque Era.
New York: W. W. Norton, 1947.   489 p.
```

a. Author's name. The author's name as given on the title page is usually the correct form. But if the title page omits names or initials normally associated with the author, or required to establish identity, supply them from some other reliable source. (The strictest bibliographic usage encloses such emendations in brackets.)

```
Stendhal [Marie-Henri Beyle]. . . .
   or
[Beyle, Marie-Henri] Stendhal. . . .
Glebov, Igor [recte Boris Vladimirovich
   Asafiev]. . . .
   or
Asafiev, B[oris] V[ladimirovich], [pseud. Igor
   Glebov].  Russian Music from the Beginning of
   the Nineteenth Century. Translated from the
   Russian by Alfred J. Swan. Published for the
   American Council of Learned Societies by J. W.
   Edwards, Ann Arbor, Mich., c1953.
```

Joint authorship. Only the first author's name need be alphabetized.

```
Dart, Thurston, Walter Emery, and Christopher
```

> Morris. <u>Editing</u> <u>Early</u> <u>Music</u>: <u>Notes</u> <u>on</u> <u>the</u>
> <u>Preparation</u> <u>of</u> <u>Printer's</u> <u>Copy</u>. Fair Lawn,
> N.J.: Oxford University Press, 1963. 22 p.

Occasionally, where there are several authors with long names, the entry may be simplified by putting only the most important name(s), followed by "and others." The additional names may be given later in the entry, or in an annotation. For et al. (not recommended), see under rule 70 Abbreviations.

> Michel, François, and others. <u>Encyclopédie</u> <u>de</u>
> <u>la</u> <u>musique</u>. [Publié sous la direction de
> François Michel en collaboration avec François
> Lesure et Vladimir Fédorov et une comité de
> rédaction composée de Nadia Boulanger et al.]
> 3 vols. Paris: Fasquelle, 1958-61. 718; 719;
> 1023 p.
> Collaer, Paul, et al. <u>Atlas</u> <u>historique</u> <u>de</u> <u>la</u>
> <u>musique</u>. . . .

For a listing of this item by title, see rule 122.

Same author. When listing two or more titles by the same author, do not repeat the name, but put seven hyphens, followed by a period.

> Reese, Gustave. <u>Music</u> <u>in</u> <u>the</u> <u>Middle</u> <u>Ages</u>. New
> York: W. W. Norton, 1940. 502 p.
> --------. <u>Music</u> <u>in</u> <u>the</u> <u>Renaissance</u>. Revised edi-
> tion. New York: W. W. Norton, 1959. 1022 p.

No author. A few works may be said to have no author, properly speaking. The title itself is run out to the left margin, alphabetized along with the other entries. With some standard reference works, the original editor's name has now become a part of the accepted title.

> <u>Baker's</u> <u>Biographical</u> <u>Dictionary</u> <u>of</u> <u>Music</u> <u>and</u>
> <u>Musicians</u>. Fourth edition, revised and en-
> larged. New York: G. Schirmer, 1940. With
> bound-in Supplement 1949, edited by Nicholas
> Slonimsky, n.d. 1298 p.

The Performing Arts: Problems and Prospects.
  Rockefeller Panel Report on the Future of the
  Theatre, Dance, Music in America. New York:
  McGraw-Hill, 1965. 258 p.
  List of panel participants, pp. 227-29.
Tudor Church Music. 10 vols. Editorial Com-
  mittee: P. C. Buck, E. H. Fellowes, A.
  Ramsbotham, R. R. Terry, and S. T. Warner.
  London: Published for the Carnegie United
  Kingdom Trust by the Oxford University Press,
  1923-1929.

b. Title (underlined). Copy the exact wording from the title
page. In transcribing the display type to ordinary typing, some
punctuation should be added: a period at the end; a colon (some
styles prefer a semicolon) to separate the main title from a subtitle.
Capitalize the first word of title and subtitle (if any), and all principal words including nouns, pronouns, adjectives, verbs, adverbs,
and participles. Do not capitalize articles, prepositions, or conjunctions (unless the first word of title or subtitle). Italicized words in
the printed title are put in quotation marks in the typescript.

Sachs, Curt. The Commonwealth of Art: Style in
  the Fine Arts, Music and the Dance. New
  York: W. W. Norton, 1949. 404 p.
Myers, Robert Manson. Handel's "Messiah": A
  Touchstone of Taste. New York: Macmillan,
  1948. 338 p.

Foreign titles must be given in the original language. In German, capitalize the first word and *all nouns,* but not the adjectives
or other parts of speech. In French and Italian, capitalize the first
word and *proper nouns* only, except that a French title beginning
with an article may also capitalize the second word.

If you wish, put an English translation of the title, in parentheses and without underlining, after the foreign title. Information
other than the title (herausgegeben, zweite Auflage, nouvelle
édition augmentée, etc.) may be left in the original language, or in
less formal bibliographies may be rendered into English.

Schering, Arnold. Geschichte des Instrumen-
talkonzerts bis auf die Gegenwart. (History
of the Instrumental Concerto to the Present.)
Reprint of the 1927 edition. Hildesheim:
Olms; Wiesbaden: Breitkopf & Härtel, 1965.
235 p.

Brook, Barry S. La Symphonie française dans la
seconde moitié du XVIIIe siècle. 3 vols.
Paris: Institut de Musicologie de l'Univer-
sité de Paris, 1962.
Vol. I, Etude historique, 710 p. Vol. II,
Catalogue thématique et bibliographique, 732
p. Vol. III, Partitions: 6 symphonies, 2
symphonies concertantes, 232 p.

Vlad, Roman. Modernità e tradizione nella
musica contemporanea. Torino: G. Einaudi,
1955. 322 p.

c. Place: publisher. The name of the city will usually suffice.
But give the state (abbreviated) or other information if needed to
avoid vagueness or confusion. If no place is indicated, put [n.p.]
in brackets, for "no place." Or, if you can, supply the probable
place name, as [London] or [London ?], depending upon the
degree of certainty.

Allen, Warren D. Philosophies of Music History:
A Study of General Histories of Music, 1600-
1960. Gloucester, Mass.: P. Smith, 1964.
382 p.

Ethnomusicology and Folk Music: An International
Bibliography of Dissertations and Theses.
Compiled and annotated by Frank Gillis and
Alan P. Merriam. Middletown, Conn.: Published
for the Society for Ethnomusicology by the
Wesleyan University Press, 1966. 148 p.

Liszt, Franz. Briefe aus ungarischen Samm-
lungen, 1835-1866. Gesammelt und erläutert
von Margit Prahács. Budapest: Akadémiai
Kiadó, 1966. 484 p.

Where several place names appear on the title page, select the place representing the publisher's headquarters, or the place from which the work is known to have been issued.

Einstein, Alfred. <u>Mozart: His Character, His
   Work</u>. Translated by Arthur Mendel and Nathan
   Broder. New York: Oxford University Press,
   1945. 492 p.
The title page lists London, New York, Toronto. The reverse of
the title page in the copy seen specifies "Oxford University Press,
New York, Inc." and indicates "Printed in the United States of
America."

Where a work is issued jointly by two or more publishers, it is
usually sufficient to give the publisher primarily responsible.

Naylor, Edward Woodall. <u>An Elizabethan Vir-
   ginal Book</u>. London: J. M. Dent, 1905. 220 p.
The title page gives "London: J. M. Dent & Co. / New York:
E. P. Dutton & Company." The printer's colophon on p. 220,
"Turnbull and Spears, Printers, Edinburgh," suggests that the
British publisher was primarily responsible.

Where a work is issued separately, by agreement between two
or more publishers, give the publisher of the copy actually used.
If you have seen *both* versions, include them in your entry. An
alternate version not seen may be mentioned in an annotation.

Deutsch, Otto Erich. <u>The Schubert Reader: A
   Life of Franz Schubert in Letters and Docu-
   ments</u>. Translated by Eric Blom. New York:
   W. W. Norton, 1947. xxxii, 1040 p.
   Published in England as <u>Schubert: A Documen-
   tary Biography</u>. London: J. Dent, 1946. A re-
   vised and augmented version of <u>Franz Schubert:
   Die Dokumente seines Lebens</u>. 2 vols.
   Munich, 1913–14.
Donington, Robert. <u>The Interpretation of Early
   Music</u>. London: Faber and Faber, 1963. New
   York: St. Martin's Press, 1966. 605 p.

Give enough of the publisher's name to insure ready identification. *The, Company, Brothers, Ltd.*, etc., may be omitted. However, give *Co., Press, Verlag* when needed to complete the sense. Unusual designations should be given verbatim.

Boston: Boston Music Co.
New York: American Book Co.
New York: Free Press of Glencoe
Paris: Presses Universitaires de France
Zürich: Rhein-Verlag
Wien: Oesterreichischer Bundesverlag
Monaco: L'Oiseau Lyre
Lyon: Editions du Sud-Est

If the publisher's name is unknown, give place and date, separated by a comma. (This may be a confession that you have not seen the book. Explain!)

```
Avison, Charles.  An Essay on Musical Expres-
    sion.  London, 1752.  Not available for the
    present study.
```

If careful inspection actually reveals no publisher, give a warning in brackets: . . . Paris: [no publisher given] . . .

In rare cases, where the author himself has published the work: . . . Author . . . (French: Auteur; German: Selbsverlag)

If no place is given: . . . n.p. [stands for "no place"].

d. Date. (See also 113g Edition used.) Check both title page and reverse of title page before settling on the date to be given. If there is no date, put n.d. (stands for "no date"). Or find the date in some reliable bibliographic reference work and supply it in the usual way. Or, through your own detective efforts, determine the exact date [1927] or approximate date [ca. 1927] and supply it in brackets. (ca. stands for circa, "approximately.")

e. Pages. Give total number of pages in the work, normally the last Arabic page number (which may be on the last page of an appendix or index). If introductory matter is important or extensive, give number of pages involved (usually in small Roman numerals).

```
Hopkinson, Cecil.  A Bibliography of the Musical
```

<u>and</u> <u>Literary</u> <u>Works</u> <u>of</u> <u>Hector</u> <u>Berlioz</u>. With
Histories of the French Music Publishers Con-
cerned. Printed for the Edinburgh Biblio-
graphical Society, 1951. xix, 205 p.
Introduction, pp. ix-xix, has illuminating
commentary on the bibliographer's problems.

For a fuller description, mention illustrations, plates, musical
examples, facsimiles; account for bound-in or accompanying matter that is separately paged, or unpaged.

Collaer, Paul. <u>A</u> <u>History</u> <u>of</u> <u>Modern</u> <u>Music</u>.
Translated from the French by Sally Abeles.
Cleveland: World Publishing Co., 1961. 414
p.; 48 p. (unnumbered) musical examples bound-
in between pp. 400 and 401.

Schering, Arnold. <u>Geschichte</u> <u>der</u> <u>Musik</u> <u>in</u>
<u>Beispielen</u>. Leipzig: Breitkopf & Härtel, 1931.
Reprinted, New York: Broude, 1950. 481 p.;
commentary and indexes [in German], 35 p. in
pocket.

The following samples are from actual book-review descriptions:

. . . 165 p., music, illus. . . . xlv, 1031 p.,
ports., facsims. [i.e., portraits, facsimiles].
. . . vi, 463 p., music, glossary. . . . 213 p.,
illus., music, plates, bibl. . . . xxi, 759 p.,
music examples. . . . 339 p.; paper [i.e.,
paperback].

For very accurate bibliographic description, bracket a "blind
folio" (printer's term for a page that is counted, even though it
does not bear a page number).

. . . Introduction, pp. [v]-viii; errata p.
[36].

f. Editor, translator. Where a responsible *author* can be found,
list the entry by author, and put "Edited by" after the title. But
where the editor is mainly responsible for a work (as for a collection or anthology) begin the entry with the editor's name.

Wagner, Richard. The Letters of Richard Wagner:
The Burrell Collection. Edited with notes by
John N. Burk. New York: Macmillan, 1950.
665 p.

French, Richard F., editor. Music and Criti-
cism: A Symposium. Cambridge, Mass.: Harvard
University Press, 1948. 181 p.
Papers read at a symposium on music criticism
held at Harvard University in May, 1947. Con-
tains introductory remarks by Archibald T.
Davidson, and papers by E. M. Forster, Roger
Sessions, Edgar Wind, Olga Samaroff, Virgil
Thomson, Otto Kinkeldey, Paul Henry Lang, and
Huntington Cairns.

Translations. Give original author's name, exact title of the
translation, and "Translated by." The language from which the
translation was made may be indicated. If desired, title and publication information for the original version may be given in an
annotation. (Cf. *The Schubert Reader,* rule 113c.)

Bach, Carl Philipp Emanuel. Essay on the True
Art of Playing Keyboard Instruments. Translated from the German and edited by William J.
Mitchell. New York: W. W. Norton, 1949. 449
p.

g. Edition used. An edition later than the first should be properly designated. Any changes in content, editorship, number of
volumes, etc., should be mentioned *after* the edition number. A
reissue, printing, or *reprinting* does not count as an edition. For example, an edition "published with new material" in 1927, *reissued*
in 1935, and *reprinted* in 1936 and 1937, still belongs under 1927
from the standpoint of content. If you wish to be exact, search the
verso of the title page and give the date of the edition *and* reprint
used.

Forsyth, Cecil. Orchestration. Second edition.
New York: Macmillan, 1935. Reprinted 1946.
530 p.

Riemann, Hugo. <u>Musik-Lexikon</u>. 11th ed., in 2
    vols. Edited by Alfred Einstein. Berlin:
    Max Hesse, 1929.
<u>The</u> <u>Letters</u> <u>of</u> <u>Mozart</u> <u>and</u> <u>His</u> <u>Family</u>. Chrono-
    logically arranged, translated and edited with
    an introduction, notes and indexes by Emily
    Anderson. Second edition, prepared by A.
    Hyatt King and Monica Carolan. 2 vols. Lon-
    don: Macmillan; New York: St. Martin's Press,
    1966. xlv, 510; xxv, 515-1032 p. The 1st
    ed. in 3 vols. appeared in 1938.
Strunk, Oliver. <u>Source</u> <u>Readings</u> <u>in</u> <u>Music</u> <u>His-</u>
    <u>tory</u> <u>from</u> <u>Classical</u> <u>Antiquity</u> <u>through</u> <u>the</u>
    <u>Romantic</u> <u>Era</u>. New York: Norton, 1950. 919 p.
    Reissued in 5 vols., 1965. 190; 169; 214;
    166; 163 p. [each vol. paged separately];
    paper.

Any appreciable lapse of time between the appearance of the
original edition and the edition used should be mentioned in an
annotation.

Hawkins, John. <u>A</u> <u>General</u> <u>History</u> <u>of</u> <u>the</u> <u>Science</u>
    <u>and</u> <u>Practice</u> <u>of</u> <u>Music</u>. New edition, with the
    author's posthumous notes. 3 vols. London:
    Novello, 1853.
    First appeared in 1776.
Mozart, Leopold. <u>A</u> <u>Treatise</u> <u>on</u> <u>the</u> <u>Fundamentals</u>
    <u>of</u> <u>Violin</u> <u>Playing.</u> Translated by Editha
    Knocker. London: Oxford University Press,
    1948. 231 p.
    Originally published as <u>Versuch</u> <u>einer</u> <u>gründ-</u>
    <u>lichen</u> <u>Violinschule</u>, Augsburg, 1756.

h. Volumes. If the title as given covers more than one volume,
give the number of volumes in Arabic numerals after the title (or
after the number of the edition—rule 113g). If the volumes appeared in different years, give the inclusive years of the first and
last volumes as publication date.

Bücken, Ernst, editor. <u>Handbuch</u> <u>der</u> <u>Musikwis-</u>
<u>senschaft.</u> 13 vols. Potsdam: Propyläon
Verlag, 1927-31. Reprinted, 13 vols.-in-9;
New York: Musurgia, n.d.
Newman, Ernest. <u>The</u> <u>Life</u> <u>of</u> <u>Richard</u> <u>Wagner.</u> 4
vols. New York: Alfred A. Knopf, 1933-1946.

Where each volume has a special title or subtitle of its own, it
may be worth while to list these in an annotation, with individual
dates in parentheses.

Hughes-Hughes, Augustus. <u>Catalogue</u> <u>of</u> <u>Manu-</u>
<u>script</u> <u>Music</u> <u>in</u> <u>the</u> <u>British</u> <u>Museum.</u> 3 vols.
London: British Museum, 1906-9. I, Sacred
Vocal Music, 615 p. (1906). II, Secular Vocal
Music, 961 p. (1908). III, Instrumental Mu-
sic, Treatises, etc., 543 p. (1909).

i. Series. If the volume used is part of a series, include the series
title (and number, if any) in the entry. Such series information
may be put in parentheses, without underlining.

Kagen, Sergius. <u>Music</u> <u>for</u> <u>the</u> <u>Voice:</u> <u>A</u> <u>Descrip-</u>
<u>tive</u> <u>List</u> <u>of</u> <u>Concert</u> <u>and</u> <u>Teaching</u> <u>Material.</u>
(The Field of Music, Vol. III.) New York:
Rinehart, 1949. 507 p.
Spiess, Lincoln B. <u>Historical</u> <u>Musicology:</u> <u>A</u>
<u>Reference</u> <u>Manual</u> <u>for</u> <u>Research</u> <u>in</u> <u>Music.</u>
(Musicological Studies, 4.) Brooklyn, N.Y.:
Institute of Medieval Music, 1963. xiii, 294
p.

B. Periodicals, Encyclopedias, Collections

114 Periodicals, standard entry

In its simplest form, the entry should contain: Author's last
name, *comma*, given names, *period*. Title of article, in quotation
marks, *comma*, name of periodical, underlined, *comma*, volume
number in Roman numerals [*no comma*] year, in parentheses,
comma, inclusive pages, *period*.

Grout, Donald Jay. "Some Forerunners of the
Lully Opera," Music and Letters, XXII (1941),
1-25.

For periodicals which are ordinarily bound in consecutively
paged annual volumes, omit the "number" (e.g., Vol. IV, No. 3).
But for issues which are not consecutively paged throughout a
year, or which offer other complications, give date of issue and
any other clarifying information. (Cf. rule 81.)

Pike, Alfred. "The Discoveries and Theories of
Julian Carrillo, 1875-1965," Inter-American
Music Bulletin [Pan American Union, Washing-
ton, D.C.], September, 1966, No. 55, pp. 1-4.

a. Variant. Some writers prefer an Arabic numeral for the volume; it must always be separated from the inclusive pages by a
colon.

. . . 37 (1965): 14-36.

b. Author unknown. If no author is given (as with some news
articles), begin the entry with the title. *Anonymous* is used only
where the author has some special reason for hiding his identity,
such as the candid or critical nature of his article.

"Ballet Boom Continues," Musical America, Janu-
ary 1, 1956, p. 4.
[Anonymous.] "Countryville: School Music
Frontier; An Experience in Pioneering," Music
Educators Journal, XXXIX (1952), 26-27.

115 Encyclopedias, collections

Where the author of the specific article is known, treat as a combination of periodical and book entry, with page reference in
parentheses at the end.

Hipkins, George. "Harpsichord," in Grove's Dictionary of Music and Musicians. Third edition, edited by H. C. Colles. New York: Macmillan, 1927-28. (Vol. II, pp. 543-47.)

Note the inclusion of "in," "Vol.," and "pp." in this situation.

Dale, Kathleen. "The Piano Music," in The Music of Schubert. Edited by Gerald Abraham. New York: W. W. Norton, 1947. (Pages 111-148.)

Haas, Robert. "Die Oper im 18. Jahrhundert," in Handbuch der Musikgeschichte. Edited by Guido Adler. Second edition, in 2 vols. Berlin: Max Hesse, 1930. (Vol. II, pp. 718-68.)

In this case, the editor is put before the edition because Guido Adler edited *both* the first and second editions.

Koechlin, Charles. "Evolution de l'harmonie: période contemporaine, depuis Bizet et César Franck jusqu'à nos jours," in Lavignac, Encyclopédie de la musique, Part II, Vol. 1. Paris: Delagrave, 1925. (Pages 591-760.)

Begin the entry with the book title if (a) the article referred to is unsigned; (b) several articles are cited from the same source, none of them sufficiently important to merit a separate entry; (c) the article is signed by several authors, so that it would be cumbersome to include all their names, or to determine responsibility for any single statement.

Baker's Biographical Dictionary of Musicians. Fifth edition, completely revised by Nicolas Slonimsky. New York: G. Schirmer, 1958. Article, "Riemann, Hugo."

International Cyclopedia of Music and Musicians. Eighth edition, edited by Nicolas Slonimsky. New York: Dodd, Mead, 1958. Articles on Canon, Counterpoint, Double Counterpoint, Double Fugue, Episode, Fugue, and Invertible Counterpoint.

Grove's Dictionary of Music and Musicians. Fifth edition, edited by Eric Blom. New York: St Martin's Press, 1955. Article, "Singing." (Vol. VII, pp. 801-814.)

Note: This article was begun by William H. Daly, revised and continued by Mollie Sands, and further added to by Sydney Northcote—all of which is too cumbersome for a bibliographic entry, but could be explained in an annotation if it seems important.

C. MUSIC

116   Music: editions

If you cite a composition published separately, treat as you would a book (title underlined). If you cite one composition within a collection, treat as you would an article: title of work (in quotation marks), volume title (underlined). But if your study involved all or most of the entire volume give only the volume title (underlined). If a volume used is part of a series, put the series title in parentheses.

Mention the editor's name, if known. If no publication date is given use the copyright date, as: c1927 (stands for "copyright 1927"). Use annotations freely to record pertinent information about the edition.

a. Single composition, published separately

Ravel, Maurice. <u>Pavane pour une infante dé-
funte</u>, pour piano. Paris: Max Eschig, n.d.   4
p.
Riegger, Wallingford. <u>Symphony No. 4</u>, Op. 63.
Study score. New York: Associated Music Publishers, c1960.   131 p.
Verdi, Giuseppe. <u>Requiem</u>, to the memory of
Alessandro Manzoni, for four solo voices and
chorus. Piano-vocal score. (English version
by C. L. Kenney.)   New York: G. Schirmer,
1895. 211 p.

b. One composition cited, within a volume

Bach, Johann Sebastian. "Suite II, A Minor," in
<u>Six English Suites</u>. Edited by Hans Bischoff.
Scarsdale, N.Y.: Kalmus, c1945. (Pages 20-45.)
Sweelinck, Jan Pieterszoon. "Chromatic Fan-

tasia," in Music Score Omnibus, by William J.
Starr and George F. Devine. Englewood Cliffs,
N.J.: Prentice-Hall, 1964. Part 1, Earliest
Music through the Works of Beethoven, pp. 98-
100.

c. Entire volume cited

Bach, Johann Sebastian. Six English Suites.
Edited by Hans Bischoff. Scarsdale, N.Y.:
Kalmus, c1945. 87 p.
The Bischoff edition originally appeared in
1881.
Beethoven [Ludwig van]. Klavier-Sonaten. Nach
Eigenschriften und Originalausgaben herausge-
geben von B. A. Wallner. Fingersatz von
Conrad Hansen. [Urtext.] München: G. Henle,
c1952-53. 2 vols. 283; 329 p.
Newman, William S., editor. Thirteen Keyboard
Sonatas of the 18th and 19th Centuries.
Chapel Hill: University of North Carolina
Press, 1947. 175 p.
Contains sonatas of Platti, Alberti, Neefe,
Moscheles, and others.
Schubert, Franz. Fifty Songs. (High Voice.)
Edited by Henry T. Finck. Boston: Oliver
Ditson, c1904. [xxiv], 219 p.

d. Composition within a volume, in a series

Chopin, Fryderyk. "[Fifth] Nocturne," Op. 15,
No. 2, in F-sharp major. (Complete Works,
Vol. VII, Nocturnes for Piano.) Warsaw: Chopin
Institute, c1952. (Pages 37-40; commentary,
pp. 121-22.)
Corelli, Arcangelo. "Concerto Grosso No. 3," in
Chamber Suites and Concerti Grossi. Edited by
Albert E. Wier. (Longmans Miniature Arrow
Score Series.) New York: Longmans Green, 1940.
Mozart, Wolfgang Amadeus. "Quintett," in G

minor, K. 516, for 2 violins, 2 violas, and
cello. Score. (Werke, Serie XIII, Quintette
für Streichinstrumente.) Leipzig: Breitkopf &
Härtel, 1883. Reprinted, Ann Arbor: J. W.
Edwards, 1956. (Pages 86-111.)

e. Entire volume cited, in a series

Bach, Johann Sebastian. Sechs brandenburgische
Konzerte. (Neue Ausgabe sämtlicher Werke.
Hrsg. von Heinrich Besseler. Serie VII,
Orchesterwerke, Band 2.) Kassel und Basel:
Bärenreiter, 1956. 243 p., 4 facsims.
See Commentary (Kritischer Bericht) by Hein-
rich Besseler, in separate volume. Bären-
reiter, 1956. 170 p.
Froberger, Johann Jakob. Clavierwerke: II.
(Denkmäler der Tonkunst in Oesterreich, VI.
Band, Zweiter Teil.) Vienna: Artaria, 1899.
84 p. Contains 28 suites.
Poglietti, Alessandro. Harpsichord Music.
Edited by William Earle Nettles. (The Penn
State Music Series, No. 9.) Pennsylvania
State University Press, 1966. 44 p.

117 Music: manuscripts, autographs, facsimiles

In citing a music manuscript or composer's autograph to which
you have had access, mention its location. If you used a microfilm
or photocopy, this fact should be mentioned. Published facsimiles
should be identified as such. Unpublished titles are put in quotation marks. If no formal title, describe.

Bach, Johann Christian. "Artaserse." Opera in
3 acts. Autograph score, dated 1761. London, British Museum, R. M. 22.a.18-20.
(Microfilm.)
London, British Museum, Add. 27550-54. Suites
for 4 viols with a figured bass for organ, in
parts, by John Jenkins. 5 vols. (Microfilm.)

Debussy, Claude. __Prélude à l'après-midi d'un faune__. Facsimile of the autograph particelle. Washington: Lehman Foundation, 1963. 6 sheets, large folio.

Bellini, Vincenzo. __Norma__. Facsimile della partitura autografa. 2 vols. Roma: Reale Accademia d'Italia, 1935. 147; 103 leaves, oblong folio.

Anglés, Higinio, editor. __La Música de las Cantigas de Santa Maria del Rey Alfonso el Sabio__. Vol. I. Facsimil del Códice j.b.2 de El Escorial. Barcelona: Biblioteca Central, 1964. xvi, 12, 361 plates, large folio.

118 Recordings

Information given on the recording may be edited to suit bibliographic style. Besides composer and title, give principal performing artists, issuing company, issue number.

Gibbons, Orlando. __Orlando Gibbons: Tudor Church Music__. Under the general direction of Boris Ord and Thurston Dart. The Choir of King's College Chapel, Cambridge, directed by Boris Ord. Hugh McLean, organist. Westminster XWN 18165. Jacket notes by Thurston Dart, c1956.

Mahler, Gustav. __Symphony No. 1 in D ("The Titan")__. Bruno Walter conducting the Columbia Symphony Orchestra. Columbia ML 5794. Jacket notes by Bruno Walter, c1962.

__Ustad Ali Akbar Khân: Master Musician of India.__ __Râga Chandranandan; Râga Gauri Manjari.__ Produced by James Lyons. One 12" 45 rpm stereo disc. Connoisseur Society CS 462. Descriptive notes by J. Lyons, 6 p., music, photos.

Webern, Anton von. __Anton Webern: The Complete Music__. Recorded under the direction of Robert Craft. Four 12" 33 1/3 rpm discs. Columbia

album K4L-232.   Pamphlet, 29 p., with note by
Robert Craft.

a. Tape recordings. Underline published titles. For unpublished
phonotapes, put identifying title in quotation marks and describe
sufficiently to establish physical existence and location. For more
careful library classification, the *collation* would include: number
of reels; reel size (diameter); speed, ips. (inches per second);
playing time (e.g., approx. 17 min.); tape width, if other than
standard ¼″; where applicable, stereo, and number of tracks.

Henze, Hans Werner. Five Symphonies. Berlin
    Philharmonic Orchestra conducted by Hans
    Werner Henze. Four track 7 1/2 ips. stereo
    tape, two reels. Ampex/Deutsche Grammaphon
    S-9204.
"Thirty-Seven Traditional Songs of Caithness and
    the Orkney Islands," sung by John Gow and
    George Stewart. Collected by John McLeod,
    August, 1967. Two reels. In the private col-
    lection of John McLeod.

D. Reviews, Theses, Documents

119   Reviews

The logical place to enter a review is in an annotation under
the book or music reviewed. (See models below for Ives and Newman.) However, to call special attention to a review, it may be
entered under its author's name with a cross reference to the item
reviewed. (See Schwarz.) But if you have not seen the item reviewed you must, willy nilly, describe it fully after the reviewer's
name (cf. rule 85).

Boyden, David D. The History of Violin Playing:
    From Its Origins to 1761, and Its Relationship
    to the Violin and Violin Music. London, New
    York: Oxford University Press, 1965. xxiii,
    569 p., with demonstration record.
Ives, Charles. Second Pianoforte Sonata: "Con-

cord,Mass., 1840-1860." Aloys Kontarsky,
piano; Theo Plümacher, viola; Willy Schweger,
flute. Time Records S/8005.
Reviewed by Henry Leland Clarke in Musical
Quarterly, 50 (1964): 114-15.
Newman, William S. The Sonata in the Classic
Era. Chapel Hill: University of North Caro-
lina Press, 1963. 897 p.
Reviewed by Jan LaRue in Musical Quarterly, L
(1964), 398-405.
Schwarz, Boris. Review of David D. Boyden, The
History of Violin Playing (q.v.), in Musical
Quarterly, 53 (1967): 109-22.
[q.v. stands for quod vide, "which see"—a signal to look up the
item mentioned under its own entry or heading.]

120   Theses, dissertations

Titles of unpublished theses and dissertations are put in quotation marks. Mention the academic degree involved, degree-grant-
ing institution, and date. If the thesis is available through a photocopy service, this should be indicated.

Munger, Shirley. "Gigue Types in Keyboard Music
from John Bull to J. S. Bach." Unpublished
master's thesis. University of Washington,
1950. 138 p.
Harrison, Jr., Gregory A. "The Monophonic Music
in the Roman de Fauvel." Ph.D. dissertation.
Stanford University, 1963. 591 p. (Microfilm. Ann Arbor: University Microfilms.)
Hagan, Dorothy V. "French Musical Criticism between the Revolutions (1830-1848)." Dissertation, University of Illinois, 1965. 347 p.
(Xerox copy. Ann Arbor: University Microfilms.)

121   Letters, documents

A single unpublished letter or document is usually not entered in the bibliography but is credited in a footnote at the proper place. (Cf. rule 96.) However, where such original sources are important for a particular study, they may be described in the bibliography (usually under a special heading) more fully than is possible in a footnote.

Webern, Anton von. Seven letters and forty-
    eight postcards to Josef Polnauer, on musical
    and personal matters. (1914-41.) 103 p.,
    various sizes, with four addressed envelopes.
    Originals in the Moldenhauer Archive.

For published letters and documents, it is simplest to list the entire publication and give needed details in an annotation.

Beethoven, Ludwig van. The Letters of
    Beethoven. Collected, translated, and edited
    with an introduction, appendixes, notes, and
    indexes by Emily Anderson. 3 vols. London:
    Macmillan; New York: St.Martin's Press,
    1961. liii, 484; xxxvii, 487-984; xxxiii,
    987-1090 p.
    Letter to Archduke Rudolph, dated Vienna,
    December 31, 1817, II, 724, with facsimile,
    2 p., facing pp. 720-21.
The Bach Reader: A Life of Johann Sebastian Bach
    in Letters and Documents. Edited by Hans T.
    David and Arthur Mendel. New York: Norton,
    1945. 431 p.
    Inventory of Bach's estate, pp. 191-97.

For occasional use, a shorter form might be:

Beethoven, Ludwig van. Letter to Archduke
    Rudolph, dated Vienna, December 31, 1817. In
    The Letters of Beethoven, translated by Emily
    Anderson (New York: St.Martin's Press, 1961),
    II, 724, and facsimile facing pp. 720-21.
Inventory of J. S. Bach's estate, in The Bach
    Reader, edited by Hans T. David and Arthur
    Mendel (New York: Norton, 1945), pp. 191-97.

122   Iconographic sources

Paintings, photographs, or other visual materials mentioned or described in the text are usually not listed in the bibliography. If such materials are extensive or important, they can be catalogued and described fully in an appendix. But where the references involve published reproductions in books, these can be listed in the usual way, with explanation of the iconographic matters in an annotation.

Blanton, Joseph Edwin. The Organ in Church De-
    sign. Albany, Texas: Venture Press, 1957.
    492 p.
    Elaborate photographic documentation in 550
    illustrations.
Bory, Robert. Ludwig van Beethoven: His Life
    and His Work in Pictures. Trans. from the
    French by Winifred Glass and Hans Rosenwald.
    New York: Atlantis, 1964. 228 p., illus.,
    facsims., large 4to.
Atlas historique de la musique. By Paul Collaer
    and Albert Vander Linden, with the collabora-
    tion of F. van den Bremt. Preface by Charles
    van den Borren. Paris: Elsevier, 1960. 179
    p., illus., maps, facsims., large 4to.

X

REFERENCES IN THE TEXT

123 Mention of an author

Where the arrangement of ideas in a passage in your text is primarily your own, it is sufficient to confine any credits to footnote citations. But where you are consciously abstracting, paraphrasing, or quoting (rules 169-178), be courteous and mention the author's name right in your text. The rule of academic familiarity favors the use of the last name only. (The full name will appear in your first footnote reference anyway.) But use first names or initials where necessary to distinguish between authors with identical surnames. Titles of address (Count, Rev., Sir, Dr., Professor, etc.) are optional, though it is usually in better taste to omit them.

It is seldom redundant to repeat the author's name as often as necessary to make certain that ideas are attributed to the right person. You can, however, once the name is mentioned, refer back to *the author, this author, the writer, this writer.* Avoid using any of these terms in referring to yourself. (See rule 124.)

If "the author" seems stilted (and it is indeed a rather overworked cliché), try: this (adjective if desired: noted, eminent, astute, perceptive, unreliable, discredited, etc.) biographer, critic, historian, hymnologist, annalist, analyst, essayist, lexicographer, musicologist, musicographer, theorist, educator, acoustician, etc.

124 Mention of self

In general, it is better style to avoid direct reference to yourself. When you make positive statements reporting your observations, opinions, and conclusions it is assumed that you are personally responsible for these statements unless you have specifically attributed them to someone else. Proper control of sentence construction, emphasis, flow of ideas, and citation of sources should leave no doubt in the reader's mind as to what is your own contribution and what is borrowed from someone else.

"The present writer" is the safest way of referring to yourself. By convention, it means *you*, the writer of this report, term paper, thesis, etc., and should never be used to refer to anyone else. The term "author" applies properly to the writer of a published work; therefore, avoid "the author" in referring to yourself in a typescript. (See rule 123.)

On rare occasions, in informal papers, the pronoun "I" may be used frankly and openly. In passages where the writer and the reader are following an argument in close cooperation, it is proper to use "we," meaning you (the reader) and I (the writer) collectively. Note: When using any of these terms omit quotation marks, which were here used for the reason explained in rule 46.

One means of avoiding reference to self is to shift the verb to the passive voice. Compare: The *present writer* found many instances in the later works. Many instances *are found* in the later works.

125 Mention of a composer

Give the composer's full name the first time it is mentioned in your text, and last name thereafter. It is a courtesy to give the composer's dates in parentheses after the first mention of the name, as: Alexander Glazunov (1865-1936). For lesser known composers, the parenthetical dates may even appear in the main title. Or full details may be given in a footnote.[1]

1 Born St. Petersburg, August 10, 1865; died Paris, March 21, 1936.

126 Mention of titles

When titles are mentioned in the text, the following rules should be helpful, though they are not absolutely fixed.

Underline titles of:
    books;

musical compositions (but not opus numbers);
operas;
plays, motion pictures;
long poems;
paintings, sculpture, ships;
periodicals, pamphlets, newspapers, journals.

Quote (and omit underlining, even if a foreign language) titles of:

articles;
parts, sections, chapters of books;
short musical compositions with literary titles;
essays (if less than book length);
unpublished matter.

Note: Titles of vocal compositions are normally underlined (treated as musical compositions). But titles of arias or songs being discussed as parts of a longer work (opera, oratorio, cantata, song cycle) may be quoted (treated as short poems).

Neither underline nor quote (but capitalize principal words) titles of:

movements of an instrumental composition (Introduction, Adagio, Scherzo, March to the Scaffold, etc.);
instrumental works in general, wherever underlining would seem fussy (Fifth Nocturne; Symphony No. 4, in E minor);
books of the Bible, Psalms;
institutions (Paris Conservatoire; Gesellschaft der Musikfreunde).

Note: For musical compositions, you may still underline for emphasis if you want a title to stand out within a paragraph of discussion.

127   Parenthetical references

Passing references that cannot be gracefully incorporated into the text, and are too short to deserve a footnote, may be put in parentheses in the text, as:

Harding, in *Saint-Saëns and His Circle* (p. 155), gives the circumstances of the composer's loss of his son.

Winton Dean (*Bizet*, pp. 212-13) warns us that *Carmen* as we hear it may not be as Bizet intended it.

In such cases, you will usually already have introduced the reference in some previous footnote. If the title can be omitted without confusion, give only the page reference: Harding (p. 163) . . . etc.

Common abbreviations in such parenthetical references are: Vol. (volume), Chap. (chapter), No. (number), Ex. (example), Pl. (plate), p. (page), pp. (pages), l. (line), ll. (lines) [easily confused with Arabic numerals 1 and 11 in typescript], n. (note— a footnote on the page indicated), fol. (folio), meas. (measure, measures) [mm. looks like "millimeters"]. Note the use of "sc." for either "scene" or "score": (Act III, sc. i) . . . (p. 14, sc. 2, meas. 1-3), or else (p. 14, 2: 1-3). (Cf. rule 92a.)

128 References to measures

Where a musical composition has appeared in several editions, reference to page numbers may confuse a reader using a different edition. (Note the importance of citing the *edition used!*) Measure numbers (or rehearsal letters or numbers) printed in the music may be used as auxiliary landmarks, as:

The stringendo (meas. 335-37) into the Allegro con anima (meas. 338) . . . etc.

Measures 2-5 after rehearsal number 3 . . . etc.

Where no such landmarks are imprinted, count as "one" the first (full) measure on the page indicated, as: . . . p. 13, meas. 5, and p. 14, meas. 11-13.

Alternatively, if there is more than one system ("score") per page, give page, *comma*, system, *colon:* measure number on that particular system, as: . . . p. 23, 4: 6-7; p. 24, 1: 1-6.

If convenient, give further landmarks, as: . . . at the *molto cresc.* (p. 5) . . . on p. 7, at *a tempo (più calmo)* . . . p. 8, meas. 15 (at the *ff*) . . . meas. 4 (dim. 7th chord on A sharp).

129 Bracketed references

Though not generally recommended, bracketed references are sometimes used consistently to avoid footnotes. The items in the bibliography are numbered consecutively. The reference is given by enclosing in brackets, at the proper place in the text, the item number in the bibliography (underlined), followed by a comma and the page number, as:

```
Both Cooper [3, 46] and Vallas [16, 175-77]
mention . . . etc.
```

Anyone who has seen such bracketed references in *microfilmed* materials realizes what a nuisance they can be.

130   Cross references: above, below

Use "above" and "below" in preference to the Latin *supra* and *infra*. Page references to other portions of the typescript can, and should, usually be avoided. Every such cross reference teases the reader to turn back or ahead, and this can be very distracting unless there is a very good reason for it.

Instead, put "we have seen that . . ." or "we shall see that . . ." and give a *brief résumé* of the point previously made, or to be made later. Such a re-summation (or pre-summation) of important points often helps to organize a paper by providing connectives and showing the broader trends of the discussion. In a thesis, this principle may be combined with a chapter reference, as: "In Chapter II it was shown that . . ." or "We shall discuss in Chapter VII the implications . . ." or "In Appendix A. . . ."

See Section XI, Illustrative Material, regarding references in your text to your musical examples, figures, plates, tables, etc.

XI

ILLUSTRATIVE MATERIAL

131 Verbal matter

For direct quotations see rules 172-178. Sometimes there may be verbal matter (which would be set in smaller type in a book) to be included in the typescript to illustrate or exemplify some point in the discussion. Such matter may be typed with single spacing and set off from the main text (cf. rule 19). For example:

a series of definitions;

a long series of items that would be tiresome or out of place in the double-spaced text;

a lengthy abstract;

a model of verbal procedure;

the complete text of a vocal composition, whether poetry or prose;

two texts placed in parallel columns for comparison.

If desired, such a "verbal illustration" (for that is what it essentially is) may be given a centered heading to make clear its purpose and to avoid its being mistaken for a long direct quotation. Leave a triple space above such a heading, and a double space between the heading and the single-spaced matter. Do not use the formal identification "Example" or "Table" in such headings. (Cf. rules 132, 135.)

a. Poetry. For brief quotations, see rule 47. Four or more lines of poetry are best set off from the text as single-spaced verbal illustration, approximately centered on the page. Where the words have been taken directly from a musical score, there may be a problem in determining the beginning of each new line of verse. If possible, consult a source that shows the poem printed *as poetry.*

b. Lengthy titles. Long titles of old books or musical editions are sometimes given because of their documentary interest. They may be set off from the text and treated as verbal illustrations: lay out the title, centered, with double spacing, to conform as closely as possible with the original in typography and distribution of lines. Omit conventional title underlining, and italicize only words that are in italics in the original title.

Alternatively, put the title in paragraph form (i.e., not centered), with slash marks / to indicate the separation of lines / in the original.

132 Musical examples

Musical examples should be neatly drawn in ink (in theses, use India ink), provided with captions, and centered on the page. Be careful not to extend into the margins. Number the musical examples consecutively throughout the paper or thesis, and make sure to refer to each and every example at some place in your text!

When an example is mentioned in your discussion (Example 1), the reader expects to find it later on the same page, or else on the page immediately following. (Example 2.) When the examples are thus cued into the text, it is quite proper to finish the sentence or paragraph before actually inserting the example. Therefore, do not insert examples *too soon.* If one has to go looking for them,

Example 1. Victoria, Motet "O Vos Omnes," meas. 11-16

Example 2. Motive transformations

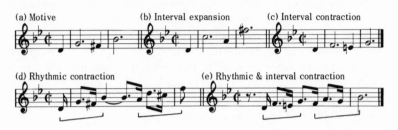

it is more natural to turn ahead one or more pages, rather than to turn back.

Examples are for the purpose of *illustrating* your verbal discussion, which must be complete and satisfying in itself. A common misconception is that you can turn the reader loose on the example and expect him to do *your* work for you.

a. The caption. (Cf. rule 32.) The caption should contain the example number and brief identification. That is, each example, together with its caption, should make some kind of sense by itself, independently of the text. Musical quotations should usually bear the name of the composer, title of the composition, indication of which movement (if more than one), and measure numbers. If the source is not well known, give a parenthetical citation at the end of the caption (cf. rule 104).

b. Reference marks. Where desirable, signs or symbols (letters, numbers, brackets, graphic markings, etc.) may be inserted into the musical example as precise points of reference for features deserving attention. Such landmarks will normally be explained along with the verbal discussion in the body of your text. Alternatively, type the explanation of symbols with single spacing directly below the example.

c. Inked-in examples. Ideally, a musical example would be neatly hand drawn in India ink directly on the typing paper, with comfortable spacing above and below—a procedure involving some skill and practice!

d. Pasted-in examples. Note: Pasted-in examples are usually not acceptable in theses. But with suitable precautions, paste-up masters may be used for duplication, as with the Xerox process. (See

Section XII, Duplicating, Photocopying, and Printing Processes.)

For reports and term papers: make up all the musical examples *first*, neatly drawn on staff paper, being careful not to exceed 6½ inches in width. Trim away the excess staff paper. When you come to a place for a musical example in the typescript, type the caption so that it will begin vertically flush with the left edge of the (centered) example. After the paper is removed from the typewriter, attach the example in the space left for it, using paper cement. If paper cement is used sparingly, examples may be "lifted" from a preliminary draft and reset in the final version of the typescript.

e. Cumulated or full-page examples. Where there is a large number of examples, or the individual examples are extended, they may be collected from time to time onto a "page of examples" (numbered consecutively along with the rest of the typescript) on appropriate staff-ruled pages. A page of examples should be placed immediately after that page of text on which mention is made of the first of the examples. In theses, the proper margins should be left blank. In informal typescripts, where staff-ruled notebook paper is used, be sure to leave adequate left margin.

Examples requiring more than six inches of width (up to nine inches) may be placed "broadside." That is, to inspect the example, the page is turned clockwise, so that the top of the example (with liberal space above) is toward the normal left margin.

133   Figures

A "figure" is a diagram, drawing, or pictorial representation included in the text for illustrative purposes. In a report dealing with the history of instruments, for example, the illustrative material might consist largely of figures. Figures should be numbered consecutively and provided with legends (rule 33). The figure number and legend are placed *below* the figure.

134   Plates

A "plate" is a page that is reserved entirely for illustrative material. (In books, the plates are commonly on a different quality of paper from that used for the text.) Typically, a plate will consist of a photostatic reproduction or photographic print of full-page size, or of elaborate hand-drawn material. Or several figures may be laid out together so as to fill up a page.

Plates are numbered consecutively with Roman numerals. At the same time, they may be paged consecutively with the text in Arabic numerals, so that the position of the plate in the typescript is never in doubt. (A "frontispiece" is placed immediately before the first page of text.) Each plate should bear a plate number and legend (rule 33), and the numbers and legends are carried in a table of illustrations (after the table of contents) at the beginning of the typescript.

Where several figures appear on the same plate, these should be given individual figure numbers and legends, for ready identification.

A broadside plate (turned sideways) should have its top toward the normal left margin.

135   Tables

A "table" is an arrangement in condensed form of data, statistics, etc., often in parallel columns. (For Table of Contents, see rule 155.) Tables are typically included to provide detailed evidence to support or illustrate matters discussed in the main text. A table should bear a caption (rule 32), be centered on the page, and be set off from the main text with suitable space above and below. If there are several tables in the typescript, begin each caption with a table number (Roman), as: Table I. . . . Table II. . . . etc.

For a simple table, single or double spacing is optional, whichever appears neatest and most readily legible. For a more complex table, effective layout is essential, with suitable vertical and horizontal spacing and alignment, and possibly even ruled lines to set off various columns and divisions. Where a table occupies an entire page, the page should be numbered (Arabic) consecutively with the rest of the typescript. Tables requiring extra width may be set broadside, with the top of the table toward the normal left margin.

XII

DUPLICATING, PHOTOCOPYING,

AND PRINTING PROCESSES

What if more than one copy of the typescript is needed? The simplest procedure is to type one or more carbon copies along with the original. Or one can type on special "master" sheets for *duplicating* by a spirit process such as Ditto, or on stencils for mimeographing. Various *photocopying* processes now widely used are convenient, and some of them produce copies far superior to the older so-called duplicating methods. For those who hope to have material printed, a section is here included· on *printing processes* explaining some of the terminology.

The information here given does not pretend to be complete, or even up to date. The technologies of "reprography" (making reproductions) are represented by a bewildering number of manufacturers and product trademarks which change constantly. But at least brief descriptions of a few typical processes, as of the date of this writing, may serve as a point of departure for making further local inquiry. Consult the experts, whether these be attached to some institution with which you are connected, or found through the Yellow Pages under *Duplicating, Photo Copying,* or *Printers.*

136   Carbon copies

Use a good quality of carbon paper, and replace frequently with fresh sheets, possibly every ten pages. The number of good, legible copies obtained depends upon the weight of paper used (rule 11) and whether a manual or electric typewriter is employed. For more than two or three copies, the correcting of typing errors becomes burdensome, and the inserting and removing of carbon sheets is distracting and time consuming.

A. DUPLICATING

137 Ditto

The active principle is a transferable dye. The master consists of a glazed typing sheet backed with a sheet impregnated with dye. (Remove the protective tissue before typing, and reinsert it after typing to avoid smudges in handling.) The action of the typewriter keys (or for illustrative matter a drawing stylus) transfers a layer of the dye onto the back of the glazed sheet to provide a reverse image of the page of typing. In the machine, copy paper is first dampened with a spirit solvent and then brought into contact with the reverse image, removing enough dye to form a print. Purple dye is ordinarily used, and copies can be run until the master sheet is exhausted. Depending upon the skill of the typist and the operator, anywhere from 20 to 200 good copies can be obtained. The copies fade upon prolonged exposure to light, and this method is not recommended for permanence.

138 Mimeographing

The active principle is a transferable pigment (ink) supplied continuously from a reservoir. The master consists of a stencil (a fibrous tissue with a waxy substance impervious to ink), an interleaving tissue (remove before typing), and a stiff backing sheet. Before typing, disengage the ribbon by moving the control lever to "stencil" position. (And clean the type thoroughly!) The typing (or drawing with a stylus) removes the protective coating so that, in the machine, ink will flow through the stencil onto the copy paper. Considering the cost of stencils, mimeographing is worth while only for longer runs such as, say, 50 to 1,000 copies. The special copy paper is unattractive, but otherwise the results are neat and permanent.

B. Photocopying Processes

139 Varieties of Photocopying

The following are all "black line" processes resulting in black-on-white copies. (Blueprint processes are not here discussed.) Individual trade-marked processes depend upon various combinations of the following factors:

a. Copies may be made (1) from an *original* (e.g., normal typed pages on regular paper, or in some cases even pages in books or magazines), either directly or by means of an "intermediate master" produced by the machine; or else (2) from a *master* typed on translucent paper (variously called vellum, tracing paper, etc.).

b. The active principle may be (1) photostatic (involving light sources only), or (2) electrostatic (involving the transfer to copy paper of latent electrostatic images).

c. The copy paper may be (1) ordinary paper, or (2) sensitized paper.

d. If special copy paper is used, it may be sensitized with (1) silver halide, or (2) diazonium salts, or (3) zinc oxide.

e. The material used to "develop" the copied image may be (1) liquid, or (2) gaseous, or (3) entirely dry.

f. The copy paper may be supplied by the machine (1) as individual sheets, or (2) from a long continuous roll.

g. The apparatus may be (1) fairly large, or (2) about the size of a desk, or (3) table-top size.

140 Xerox

The desk-size Xerox 914 Copier (The Xerox Corp.) employs the electrostatic principle and operates as follows. The original (i.e., the material to be copied) is placed face down on a scanning glass and the image reflected onto an electrically charged selenium coating on a revolving drum. The properties of selenium are such that where light strikes it the charge is dissipated into a metallic backing, while the darkened portions retain a latent electrostatic image. This image is "developed" by tumbling over it a dry powder containing carbon black and a resin binder, which adheres only to the charged portions of the plate. As the drum revolves, the resulting developed image is transferred to copy paper, to which it is permanently fused in the final step of the process.

The machine can copy book and magazine pages as well as typescript pages or other single-sheet documents up to size 9 x 14. Copies are on individual sheets of ordinary paper. (The operator may also be able to produce vellum masters from opaque originals.)

Regarding musical examples, see rule 141a.

One disadvantage of Xerography (from the Greek words *xeros,* "dry," and *graphein,* "to write") is that one cannot reproduce solid black areas or the heavier tones of halftone illustrations (rule 151).

141   Bruning Copytron 2000

(The Charles Bruning Co.) This machine also employs the electrostatic principle. The original (any single-sheet document up to size 11 x 17) is fed into the machine through rollers and moves synchronously with the copy paper, which is coated with zinc oxide in a resin binder. Light is reflected from the original and focused onto the copy paper, leaving a latent electrostatic image. The image is developed by tumbling over it a dry powder containing dye and binders, and this material is then fused into the paper. An exposure adjustment on the machine makes it possible to regulate the density of the copy, and this process will reproduce solid black areas and halftones.

There are many other electrostatic copiers on the market using zinc oxide copy paper. A few names of manufacturers at random are: A. B. Dick Co.; American Photocopy Equipment Co. [Apeco]; Dennison Mfg. Co.; SCM Corp.; Pitney-Bowles, Inc.; Savin Business Machines Corp.

a. Musical examples, electrostatic process. The Xerox and Bruning processes described above reproduce whatever is presented for copying. For musical examples (rule 132), prepare "paste-up" masters as explained in rule 132d. The black-line copies (as many as needed) will all be uniform and actually neater than the original. In lieu of paper cement, one may use invisible tape for paste-up. (Recommended: Scotch Brand Magic Mending Tape

110

No. 810. This is quite transparent, and without the brownish tint of ordinary utility Scotch tape.) Other illustrative material, such as figures to accompany the text (rule 133) may also be pasted up.

142   Diazo

The so-called "diazo" photocopying process involves aniline dyes. (*Diazo*- is a combining term used in organic chemistry.) Matter to be copied is typed on translucent master sheets. These are fed into a machine which shines ultraviolet light through the master onto sensitized paper coated with a mixture of two ingredients: a light-sensitive diazonium salt, and one of various kinds of "color couplers." The diazo material is neutralized where the light strikes, but remains active where darkened by the pattern on the master. When developed in ammonia (liquid or gaseous), the active diazo material combines chemically with the color coupler to form an aniline dye. Depending upon the substances used in the copy paper, copies may be "black line" or some other color as selected.

The Charles Bruning Co., besides electrostatic copiers (rule 141), makes diazo machines such as the Bruning Printmaster Model 820. The Ozalid trademark (General Aniline & Film Corp.) is so well known as to be often taken as synonymous with photocopying from translucent masters. The Tecnifax Corp. also supplies diazo equipment.

Vellum or tracing paper for making masters may be obtained at office-supply stores in sizes 8½ x 11, or 11 x 17. It is important that the typing or drawing be dense black (avoid blues). Use a fresh ribbon (medium to intense), and insert a reversed carbon sheet (black or yellow) behind the master sheet. The idea is to obtain a carbon deposit on both the front (ribbon) and back (carbon paper) sides, to produce a sufficiently opaque image for good quality prints. For drawings and musical examples use India ink; or trial and experience may show that certain kinds of pencils will give good results.

Note: Copies made with the diazo process tend to curl and deteriorate unless a good quality of paper is used. For theses, some librarians specify 24 lb., 100 per cent rag content paper.

a. Musical examples, diazo process. Staff-lined translucent music paper may be used to prepare musical examples. There may be problems, though, in matching music vellum, typing vellum, ink (or pencil), and typewriter ribbon to secure reasonably uniform density in the printed copies. Where there is doubt, make up a sample master to run through the machine as a test.

To insert a musical example in a typed page, trim the example to size and fit it into a window of exactly the same size, cut into the typing vellum. Secure in place with Scotch Tape No. 810. If typing and musical example are black enough, the tape will not show in the prints. But if the operator has to overexpose to make your material show up, the tape may cast an undesirable shadow.

143　Office copiers

Various handy devices of table-top size are used in the business world for making a few quick copies, but these are not recommended where elegance and permanence are desired, or where there is a long run of pages to be copied.

Verifax employs a two-stage process. The original is fed into the machine, which first makes an intermediate negative called a matrix. The matrix is run through a developing solution, and in the second stage copies (up to five or six) are printed from it on ordinary paper. The matrix cannot be saved, as it deteriorates rapidly.

Thermofax is a single-step dry method for copying. The original is brought into contact with special heat-sensitive paper and exposed to infra-red light within the machine. The black places in the original transmit heat through to the sensitized paper, producing a positive image. Any number of copies can be run, within reason.

144　Photography

One should not overlook amateur or professional photography as a source of illustrative material. The kind of light-sensitive substance used (silver halide) distinguishes photographic and photostatic processes from other kinds of photocopying. Enlargements of photographs can be treated as plates (rule 134), and should be printed on paper large enough to be trimmed to size 8½ x 11 with proper margins. So-called 8 x 10 prints (the picture is actually about 7 x 9) will do, though they crowd the left and right margins.

Or a so-called 5 x 7 enlargement can be printed up centered on the page with generous margins. If necessary, smaller prints could be attached to the typing paper with a good adhesive, but this is not particularly recommended.

The amateur photographer who owns, or can borrow, enlarging equipment may be able to make his own illustrative plates.

145   Photostat

Photostat machines (Eastman Kodak Co.) use the silver halide process. The material to be copied is placed in a copy-holder and illuminated by strong lights. First a paper negative is made (white letters on black ground). If positive prints are desired, they are printed from the negative in a second stage. Because a system of prismatic mirrors is used, prints can be produced size-to-size, or enlarged, or reduced. The paper goes through the machine in a continuous roll, and has to be developed, fixed, washed, and dried like any photographic paper. Some machines require a darkroom, while others do not.

Photostat copies, because of the weight of the paper, are likely to be used as plates (rule 134).

146   Microfilm printers

Various models of Xerox Copyflo machines take rolls of 35mm or 16mm film and produce enlarged copies on a continuous roll of paper. The Xerox 1824 Printer can do this and various other copying tasks besides.

Various models of Filmac machines (Minnesota Mining & Mfg. Co.) serve as a combined microfilm reader-printer. The operator views and positions an enlarged image on a reading screen; a print is obtained by simply pressing a button.

C. Printing Processes

The three fundamental printing methods are letterpress, gravure, and lithography. One widely used adaptation of lithography is known as "offset printing." For fuller information see the Chicago *Manual of Style*.

147 Letterpress

The principle involves a raised type face to which ink is applied and from which it is transferred to paper. Except for very small hand-set jobs, the typesetting is done with a Linotype machine which produces one-line slugs automatically justified in length. The slugs are first assembled into galleys (oblong trays), and "galley proofs" are printed for inspection by the proofreader (and sometimes the author) so that corrections can be made. Newspaper galleys are usually of one-column width; page layout is determined by a makeup expert, and the galleys are assembled, or broken up and reassembled, to form the definitive pages. Book and magazine galleys are of page width; they are broken up into page lengths which are provided with page numbers and "running heads"—e.g., the book title on the left-hand (verso) page, and the title of the chapter or other subdivision on the right-hand (recto) page. Page proofs are printed for making any final corrections. At this point an index can be made if desired.

For actual printing in rotary presses, letterpress is now usually transferred to lithographic plates (rule 149).

148 Gravure

The intaglio principle is used. The image is etched into a metal plate thin enough to be curved around a cylinder in a rotary press. In the printing process, the plate is covered completely with ink and then wiped clean, leaving the etched depressions filled with ink. Paper brought into contact with the plate pulls out the ink onto the sheet. *Photogravure* and *rotogravure* are special methods for printing faithful reproductions of photographic subjects.

149 Lithography

The image to be printed is neither raised (as in letterpress) nor depressed (as in gravure) but is impressed with greasy ink on a "flat" surface. In printing, the greasy ink is continuously renewed by a roller, but the surface is kept wet so that the ink will be repelled from the the non-greasy portions, which remain clean. The principle is now widely used in offset printing. A variant known as *collotype* is sometimes used for illustrations. *Photolithography*

merely employs modern photochemical methods for producing the
lithographic plates.

150   Offset printing

The lithographic method actually produces better results when
the image is "offset" onto the paper by means of an intermediary
hard rubber blanket. In the rotary press, the litho plate revolves
on a cylinder in contact with a rubber blanket on a second cylinder,
which in turn prints the paper as it passes over a third ("impression") cylinder. The litho plate is prepared photochemically from
an original which may be printed by letterpress, or typed (electric
typewriter with carbon ribbon), or consist of illustrative material
such as photographs and drawings.

Other terms for this process are *planograph* and *lithoprint*.
An adaptation for use in office machines is called *multilith*.

151   Illustrations

These are likely to be either black line (for black-on-white
drawings or diagrams) or halftone (reproductions of photographs,
wash drawings, or anything involving different degrees of shad-
ing).

When submitting material for publication, use India ink for
black-line drawings and make them larger than needed so that
minor defects will be eliminated when they are reduced for final
reproduction.

Halftones are illustrations printed from metal plates bearing
tiny dots etched in relief. The number of dots per inch depends
upon the "screen" used in the photoengraving process: 65-line
screen is used in newspapers; 120-line screen is common in book
printing; but 133-, 150-, and even up to 400-line screen may be
used for very fine detail. The individual dots vary in size according
to the tone values (dark, shaded, or light) of the original, creating
an illusion of black where they are large and gray tones where
they are smaller.

The term "cut" (originally *woodcut*) is now loosely used to
denote any kind of printing surface bearing illustrative matter, or a
print made from it.

152   Typographic terms

In dealing with printers it is convenient to know a few technical terms such as the following.

Point. A unit of measurement, as for type sizes. There are approximately 72 points to an inch. The main text of a book is likely to be set in 12-point type (formerly called Pica), or 11-point (Small Pica), or 10-point (Long Primer), with "reduced" matter set in type a size or two smaller than the main text. The smallest type sizes (9, 8, 7, 6, or even 5 point) are hard on the eyes, while larger sizes (14, 18 [Great Primer], 24, 30, 36 point) would be used mainly for display headings (on up to 72 point, etc., for newspaper banner headlines).

Em, en. These terms are mysterious to the uninitiated. An *em* is a unit of lineal measurement equal to the point size of the type being used. Thus for 12-point type an em is 12 points, for 10-point type 10 points, and so on. An *en* is equal to one-half an em.

Different lengths of dashes are available in printing. Examples for 12-point type:

en dash (6 points), slightly longer than a hyphen;

em dash (12 points), for normal use where a dash is expected;

2-em dash (24 points), where a long dash is needed;

3-em dash (36 points), mainly used in bibliographies to indicate the same author as in the preceding item.

In typescript such fine distinctions cannot be made: see rules 39 Hyphen, 40 Dash, and 113a under Same author.

Leading. When type is set "solid" the shoulders of the types themselves provide a certain amount of space between lines. Where more space is desired for legibility or elegance, thin strips of metal the full length of a line are inserted between lines. A lead (pronounced like the metallic element) is usually 2 points thick, and matter so spaced is said to be "2 point leaded." There are also leads 1 point or 3 points thick. Where extra wide space is needed, *slugs* 6 or 12 points thick are used.

THE THESIS

Final copies of a completed thesis should be submitted as loose sheets, never bound or punched. Each copy is put into a separate manuscript-size envelope. Firmly pasted on the outside of the envelope should be an exact copy of the title page.

153 Arrangement

Note the following order of arrangement, which in general conforms to that of printed books. For theses, however, it is recommended that a preface, if any, be placed immediately preceding the main text. For local regulations which may prescribe a slightly different arrangement, consult the proper authorities.

Front matter (pages with small Roman numerals)
    title page
    table of contents
    any additional lists needed, as: plates, illustrations, figures,
        tables, musical examples
    preface (optional)
    acknowledgments (if not included in a preface)
Main text (pages with Arabic numerals)
    with suitable main divisions into chapters
Reference matter (continue Arabic page numbers through to the end) as needed:

appendix, or appendixes
glossary
musical examples (if cumulated at the end)
bibliography
index (rarely included)

A. FRONT MATTER

154 Title page

Put the title, all in CAPITALS, two inches down from the top of the page. For titles two or more lines in length, triple space between lines. The exact form of the title page is usually prescribed by local custom. Examine models of accepted theses in your library, and also consult your thesis supervisor. The title page is counted as page i, even though no numeral appears on the page. Note: It is a gross affront to submit even a first draft of your thesis for criticism without a proper title page.

155 Contents

List the headings of each major division: preface (if any); each chapter of the main text (by chapter number and chapter title); each distinct subdivision of the reference matter. After each heading listed, carry leaders . . . . . . across to a page number (in a vertically aligned column at the right margin) indicating where that heading may be found (with the same precise wording) in the typescript.

The table of contents, taken by itself, should provide a good preliminary overview of the subject, and indicate clearly how the writer proposes to organize his materials. Chapter titles should therefore be crisp and informative. Plan a sufficient number of chapters so that the table of contents will already show all of the main elements in the discussion.

The table of contents normally begins on page ii, and may extend to one or more following pages, if needed.

156 Other lists

Where it appears desirable to provide a guide to the location of illustrative material in the typescript, one or more appropriate lists (tables) may be given after the table of contents, set up in the same general form. *Plates* (photographic reproductions of full-page size) deserve a separate listing. If figures alone, or both plates and figures are used, a general heading *Illustrations* might suffice. A list of *Tables* should be provided if these are numerous or important in the typescript. *Musical examples* are not ordinarily tabulated in the front matter, though this may be done if it seems appropriate.

157   Preface (optional)

A preface, or foreword, as the term implies, is a preliminary statement which you might like to make before launching with full energy into the main subject. A preface may be somewhat less formal in tone than the main text of a thesis, and is a handy place to clear the decks for action. One might explain how one came to be involved with the subject, the experiences one has had in the research process, and which sources of information were most helpful. One can also explain how the main body of the discussion is laid out, and call attention to features of special interest, such as appendixes, useful lists provided on particular pages, and so on. Acknowledgments (without any special heading) may be incorporated into the preface, usually toward the end.

A well-written preface puts the reader into a pleasant frame of mind for plunging into the thesis proper.

158   Acknowledgments

Note that *dedications* are appropriate for published books but not for typed theses. On the other hand, it is quite proper (and rather expected) to provide a brief paragraph or two giving credit to those who have inspired or assisted you with your work on the thesis. If such credits are not included in a preface, they may be put on a special page headed ACKNOWLEDGMENTS. Maintain a restrained and dignified tone, avoiding flowery language; mention professors who have given advice, and any persons from whom you have obtained special information (as through interviews or by correspondence). Where permission has been obtained to reproduce copyrighted materials, this should be acknowledged. Librarians and such, as well as spouses, usually remain anonymous;

though one might argue that (within reason) *any* kindness received deserves some small word of thanks.

B. Main Text

159 Chapter headings

Align the top of the paper with the line scale. Drop six double spaces (two inches), and put the chapter number and chapter title, all in capitals and without terminal punctuation. If the chapter number (CHAPTER ONE, or CHAPTER I) is on a line by itself, it takes no punctuation; but if it is followed on the same line by the beginning of the chapter title, use a colon or a period. Double space all headings of two or more lines, and leave a triple space between the chapter heading and the first line of text.

A page bearing a chapter title is a "blind folio" (rule 22), without a page number at the top. (If desired, the page number may be put in the bottom margin, centered.)

The writing of convincing chapter titles is an art in itself. (Cf. rule 179 The subject and the title.)

160 Introductory chapter

The first chapter in a thesis is usually introductory in nature, providing a general orientation to the subject. One can first describe in general terms the backgrounds and nature of the subject about to be discussed; review the pertinent literature; isolate and define the specific problem that has motivated the research; explain what the writer has attempted to do, and what he thinks he has accomplished; mention the kinds of sources used, and the methods employed in arriving at conclusions. Toward the end of the chapter, one should give a brief preview, or rehearsal, of the ensuing discussion: explain briefly what is to be covered, chapter by chapter, and what further information is to be found in appendixes, glossaries, or the like, at the end.

Sometimes a preface (rule 157) is adequate for orientation, and the first chapter of the main text can plunge directly into the subject. Or one may have both a preface and an introduction, relegating the more informal loose ends to the preface.

Although the heading CHAPTER ONE: INTRODUCTION is appropriate, remember that when the reader scans your table of contents this will tell him nothing. Where possible, an introductory chapter should have a descriptive title that gives some idea of its content.

161   Chapter arrangement

One could expect perhaps four or five chapters as a minimum, and twelve to fifteen as a maximum. Each chapter represents a major subdivision of the subject treated; the chapter titles, taken successively, should form a logical framework of organization. Chapters toward the beginning of a thesis may depend somewhat more upon secondary sources and previous investigations, but as one proceeds there should be a crescendo of emphasis upon the writer's own observations and an increase in the amount of detailed evidence presented.

162   Sections within chapters

For articulation of further subdivisions within chapters, section headings (rule 29) may be used. It is usually unnecessary to assign numbers to such subdivisions. Optionally, section headings may be carried in the table of contents, typed below their respective chapter titles with generous hanging indention (rule 21).

163   Conclusions

In the research process, conclusions are what we arrive at last. But in conveying the results of our investigation to others, it is a time-saving device to let the reader know at once (toward the very beginning of the thesis) what it is we have discovered. Such a preview of results does not take the wind out of your sails. On the contrary, if you take a definite and immediate stand, the reader is likely to read with greater interest the rest of your thesis, with its detailed lines of argument and presentation of evidence.

Nevertheless, most readers would probably like to find at the end of the main text a major subdivision devoted to "conclusions," restating in condensed form the ground covered, with possible passing commentary as to how all this might influence our thinking in relation to the subject dealt with. Such a subdivision may be dignified with a chapter heading (CHAPTER X: CONCLUSIONS), or else simply given an unnumbered heading (CONCLUSIONS), as a kind of preface-in-reverse.

164 Special cases

In those rare instances where the material does not seem divisible into "chapters," some alternative system may be used. Thus, if there are only two major subdivisions of a subject, consider PART I and PART II, with liberal provision for section headings in each Part.

Sometimes the principal substance of a thesis is in musical notation, as in the case of a transcription, modern edition, or even an original composition with prefatory remarks. If the typescript portion is too brief to divide up into chapters, it may be presented as an *Introduction*, paged with small Roman numerals. The musical portion can then begin with a subsidiary title page and (Arabic) page numbers of its own.

It is technically possible to bind together a typescript (on standard paper) and a musical score (of larger page size), though some libraries may not accept this hybrid format. If a stationer can supply uncut sheets (11 x 17) of typing paper, these can be trimmed to the same size as the music paper used. Typescript on such oversize pages should be quite generous with margins.

C. REFERENCE MATTER

165 Appendixes

Any homogeneous block of material which does not fit gracefully into the main text, but which ought to be available for reference, may be put into a subdivision headed APPENDIX. There may be as many appendixes (headed APPENDIX I, APPENDIX II, etc., or APPENDIX A, APPENDIX B, etc.) as there are distinct blocks of material. Each appendix should carry a title that adequately describes its content, as: Appendix I: Chronological List of the Songs. . . . Appendix II: Translations of Song Texts. Such appendixes should be carried in the table of contents, and one must always justify their presence *somewhere* in the course of the main text.

166   Glossary

Where special or unusual terminology is an important factor in the thesis, consider bringing all such terms together into an alphabetical dictionary headed GLOSSARY, or VOCABULARY. The glossary is primarily for reference, and does not obviate the necessity for explaining terms in the main text.

If such terms are so few in number that a special glossary would seem ridiculous, they may be put instead at some appropriate place in the main text in the form of a table or a section, perhaps headed *Definitions*.

167   Cumulated musical examples

Ideally, each musical example should appear on the same page as (or on the page next following) the passage in the main text where it is first discussed. Sometimes, because of technical problems of makeup, it may be more convenient to cumulate all musical examples in a special subdivision, headed MUSICAL EXAMPLES, as reference matter. The examples must be carefully numbered and captioned (rule 132a), and cued into the text (rule 132). When reference is made to the first example (Example 1), explain in a footnote that musical examples will be found on pages . . . (give inclusive pages where one must look).

For the BIBLIOGRAPHY, see rules 106-122.

168   Index

A thesis rarely requires an index. For helpful advice on preparing book indexes, see the University of Chicago Press *Manual of Style*, pp. 211-13.

PART TWO

Writing Skills

PRELUDE

Part One dealt with the more or less mechanical aspects of style in the typescript. Part Two will attempt to deal briefly with the vehicle of communication itself, namely, literary style. Music students are likely to expend the greater part of their energies—and rightly so!—in dealing with the language of music. Only rarely does the musician have the opportunity to study and practice the skills of written English in a measure comparable, say, to the student of literature, philosophy, or history. It seems appropriate to gather together here for ready reference a few hints and suggestions—some new, some old—that may help the student improve his written communication.

The handling of extracts (i.e., direct quotations, whether single spaced or double spaced) is usually dealt with in style books as if it were something purely mechanical or perfunctory. In *Writing about Music*, it will be noted that this subject has been moved over into "writing skills," and put in third place after the vitally important questions of abstracting and paraphrasing.

The other sections can be referred to individually, as needed. Section XV, Organization of the Paper, is perhaps closest to the immediate problem of getting a paper written. For a review of the structural components of language—words, phrases, clauses, sentences, paragraphs—see Section XVI. The student who is convinced that his writing lacks sparkle, vitality, and conviction may be encouraged by looking at Section XVII, Control of Literary

Style. If the problem is how to get hold of the subject, try the review of traditional kinds of writing in Section XVIII.

Publication, like being born or getting married, is an experience each individual has to go through for himself. It seems not altogether inappropriate, however, that today's student (who may be tomorrow's author!) should have an early brief glimpse of some of the possibilities, as in Section XIX, Writing for Publication.

XIV

ABSTRACT, PARAPHRASE,
DIRECT QUOTATION

169 Rationale

Most information obtained from sources is presented in the form of an abstract or paraphrase of the original. Direct quotation should be reserved for special situations. The rapport between the writer (you) and the reader is momentarily suspended each time you direct attention to someone else's words by quoting directly. If this is done too often, or without real plan or reason, the reader will think of you as only a nonentity, or a parrot, or both.

A. ABSTRACT AND PARAPHRASE

If one's writing is to carry conviction, it ought at all times to be a direct expression of the writer's own personality. "Say it in your own words" is a magic formula that time and again cuts through whole jungles of vagueness and misunderstanding. It matters not whether one's "own words" are simple and homely, or precociously sesquipedalian (rule 215); truths have been uttered in all manner of language.

Inexperienced writers are too easily overwhelmed and seduced by the literary skill of whatever author they happen to be reading at the moment. This or that expression or turn of phrase—indeed, whole passages—are borrowed with the mistaken notion that one's own writing will benefit in the process. If, as it should, the student's research takes him through many authors, the resulting paper may be an undigested hodgepodge of styles likely to leave the discerning reader unconvinced, if not nauseated.

True, one must *learn* from the best writers. But the learning process consists, not in slavishly copying their more successful moments, but in observing their skill and know-how and trying to adapt it to our own personal idiom.

The real work horses of scholarly writing are therefore the art of abstracting and the art of paraphrasing. Or one could call them disciplines, for they require energy and self-control. The comparatively easy process of extracting direct quotations can produce spectacular results in skillful hands. Unsophisticated overuse of direct quotation, on the other hand, smothers whatever literary style one may have more quickly than wild morning-glories in a summer garden.

170 Abstract

An abstract is a condensed summary of the main gist of some longer passage, or section, or even a whole article or book. The purpose of an abstract is to generalize an attitude or a contribution. Since any abstract should be essentially in your own words, it should be fitted smoothly into your (double-spaced) main text. (An exception might be a very lengthy abstract, treated as verbal illustration—rule 131.)

The art or science of abstracting is one of the most important procedures in scholarly writing; for when the writer is not bringing into sharp focus the information and commentary provided by others, he is condensing into usable form his own digressive thinking, observation, and experience.

When you present someone else's ideas in abstract, provide a reference (rules 72-75) just as you would for a direct quotation, mentioning the inclusive pages of the whole passage abstracted. (An abstract of an entire book requires no page reference.)

Special case: Doctoral candidates are usually asked to prepare for publication an abstract of the dissertation. The whole content of a study perhaps running to hundreds of pages may need to be stated in not more than 600 words.

171 Paraphrase

A paraphrase is a free rendering or rephrasing of a passage, retaining the exact meaning but using a different wording. The purpose of a paraphrase is to reproduce the details of an argument or train of thought. The paraphrase may be longer than the original (as when the original is condensed and packed with meaning), or briefer than the original (as when the original is prolix and slow in coming to the point).

Technical words, or words possessing an exact shade of meaning, may be borrowed from the original; but the word order, sentence structure, and emphasis should be purposely altered as a test to show that you understand the *meaning* (not merely the wording) of the passage.

Paraphrasing affords an opportunity to clarify and explain the original, and to adjust the content to your own particular literary style and intentions. In "adjusting" the content, never read into a passage something that is not actually there. (The reader may look up the original!)

If you wish to interject comments of your own, you must learn to turn the paraphrase "on" and "off." It is "on" when you mention the author's name and continue as if you were retelling what he said. It is "off" when you make a positive statement that obviously conflicts with, or modifies, the original author's intentions. To turn the paraphrase back on, reintroduce either the author's name or a pronoun representing him. Indirect discourse may be helpful, as: He goes on to say that . . .

The whole purpose and nature of a paraphrase is such that it must be run into your (double-spaced) main text. Give a reference to the source, just as you would for a direct quotation or an abstract.

See also rule 105. For carrying on an argument with an author, it may be convenient to put the paraphrase in the main text, and your running commentary in a series of footnotes.

B. Direct Quotations

See also rule 131 Verbal matter, including poetry (131a) and lengthy titles (131b).

172   Spacing

There are two ways of treating direct quotations, sometimes called "extracts"—i.e., any material extracted verbatim from its source. (a) The material may be enclosed in quotation marks (rule 43) and run into the double-spaced text. (b) The material may be set off from the main text in a matter corresponding to the use of smaller type in a book: single spaced, without quotation marks, and with recessed left margin (rule 19).

Method *a* is preferable for brief quotations (up to 4-5 lines), or even for longer quotations which are frequently interrupted by your own running comments.

Method *b* is preferable when the quotation is long enough to involve possible confusion with your own text, or where it is presented as an exhibit. (The manner of introducing and crediting a quotation should always distinguish it from other kinds of verbal illustration—rule 131.)

173   Selectivity

Avoid verbatim quotation of commonplace thoughts, or long, windy passages that could be more concisely stated in your own words. (Give an abstract or paraphrase instead—rules 170, 171.) In general, the use of direct quotation is reserved for these special occasions: (a) when the statement is more concise and authoritative, coming from its author, than it could possibly be paraphrased in your own words; (b) when an extended line of close reasoning can be grasped only when the complete original text is seen; (c) when one is consistently using primary sources containing new or otherwise valuable information that ought to be recorded as fully and exactly as possible.

174   Accuracy

In general, conform exactly to the original in wording, spelling, and internal punctuation. To call attention to an inaccuracy in the original, put [sic] in square brackets after the word or statement involved. Or you may put your correction in square brackets. If you italicize words of the original for emphasis, or modernize the spelling, notify the reader. On the other hand, you may want to assure the reader of "italics in the original," or "spelling as in the original" in a footnote or in square brackets.

175   Interpolations

Use square brackets to enclose comments of your own that you wish to interpolate in quoted matter. (If the typewriter has no square brackets, put them in by hand—never use parentheses.) Thus, elucidate vague or ambiguous words not elsewhere explained: "He [Wagner] described it [his new house] in his letter of 30th September [1864] to Bülow." (In such an extreme case a paraphrase would have been better!)

On rare occasions you may have to warn the reader of "brackets in the original" and avoid using them yourself.

176   Ellipsis

A quotation can often be improved by omitting portions that are not significant, so that the main point is made with a minimum of words. Put the sign of ellipsis . . . (three spaced periods) where something has been left out. If used after a complete sentence the sign follows the sentence period. . . . The three dots are the same no matter how much, or how little, has been omitted. Exceptions: A typed line of spaced periods indicates omission of one or more lines of verse (in poetry), or one or more paragraphs (in lengthy prose quotations).

177   Opening a quotation

A direct quotation should not be plumped into the midst of one's text like some foreign substance. Provide a smooth transition. The first word of a quotation may be adjusted from capital to lower case, or from lower case to capital, to suit the situation.

Quotations run into the text as portions of your own sentences. (a) Start your own sentence and lead "directly [lower case] into the quotation." Or (b) "Start [capitalized] with the quotation," and close quotes to explain it, "continue the quotation later in the sentence if you like."

Quotations (single spaced) set off from the text. (c) If your words of introduction form a complete sentence, put a colon:

Open the quotation with a capital if it begins with what can be construed as a complete sentence.

open with lower case if there is not a complete sentence up to the first period.

. . . open with ellipsis (in more formal style) if you wish to avoid the responsibility of capitalizing where there was no capital in the original. (But if there *was* a capital in the original, no ellipsis is necessary.)

(d) But if your words of introduction lead naturally into the quotation without a break, put a comma (or no punctuation at all).

Study the following examples:

Original. Splendid as are the examples of the concerto form for string and wind instruments, it was only in the piano concertos that Mozart achieved his ideal. They are the peak of all his instrumental achievement, at least in the orchestral domain. (Alfred Einstein, *Mozart*, p. 287.)

Treatment (a). As for the piano concertos, Alfred Einstein considers that "they are the peak of all his instrumental achievement, at least in the orchestral domain."

Treatment (b). Of perhaps greater importance are Mozart's concertos for piano. "It was only in the piano concertos," according to Alfred Einstein, "that Mozart achieved his ideal."

Treatment (c). Alfred Einstein rates these works highly:

It was only in the piano concertos that Mozart achieved his ideal. They are the peak of all his instrumental achievement [longer quotation follows].

Treatment (d). Mozart is at his best in the piano concertos. For Alfred Einstein,

they are the peak of all his instrumental achievement [longer quotation follows].

178   Foreign-language quotations

Rule 64 stated that foreign words appearing in an English context should be italicized (underlined). But a quotation given entirely in the original language must *not* be underlined. Treat just as you would a quotation in English. (Cf. rule 65.)

As a general courtesy to the reader, such matter ought perhaps more properly to be presented in English translation, with the original language in a footnote or, if very extensive, in an appendix.

For very brief quotations, give the original language first, followed immediately by the English translation, in parentheses and without quotation marks.

Occasionally, where a comparison of meanings is important, the original quotation and English translation are set up side by side in parallel columns.

XV

ORGANIZATION OF THE
PAPER

179   The subject and the title

A report, term paper, or thesis represents an *intensive* result growing out of an *extensive* background of study. The subject should therefore be limited in scope, its nature clearly expressed in the title, and only such material included in the paper as is closely related to the central theme. A good paper gives the impression that its author knows much more than he has put down, but that he has purposely limited his material to give the reader a maximum of highly pertinent information in a minimum of words.

The title must be meaningful (never vague), bring the reader's attention sharply into focus, and provide a sense of direction for the entire paper. Study published titles and observe how they are constructed. Titles usually omit finite verbs and consist of one or more chief substantives (nouns or proper names) qualified by modifiers (adjectives, phrases, and possibly a subtitle). On rare occasions "verbals" (participles, gerunds, infinitives) are used as substantives and modified by adverbs. Keep titles short. Or, if they must be long, choose the chief substantives carefully, and do not tuck important issues away into obscure corners of long modifying phrases.

Formulate a title before beginning to write the paper, and bear it constantly in mind so that the paper will have a sense of direction. But after the paper is written, reconsider the title to see if it properly expresses the completed achievement, not merely what you had originally set out to do. Make up eight or ten tentative new titles, and select as definitive only that one which is most convincing.

The routine paper deserves a title and by-line just as surely as the formal report or thesis; any literary "package" should be clearly labeled as to content and manufacturer.

180   Direction, relevancy, coherence

The governing principles of organization are direction, relevancy, and coherence. A sense of *direction* in any piece of writing means a pull toward some goal. Within the first page or two the reader should already feel that the discussion is leading somewhere, that it is pointed in some definite direction. As the discussion unfolds, this sense of purposefulness creates a kind of magnetic field which pulls the reader along. Side excursions to explain supplementary matters should be either very brief or else skillfully oriented to avoid loss of momentum. The continuous queries, "Where am I going?" and "What steps do I take to get there?" can be among the most potent of organizing forces.

Journalists speak of "slant." That is, the writer attempting anything more than dull reporting views his subject from some particular angle or point of view. Scholarly writing, despite its reputation for cold objectivity, is just as likely to be slanted as any other kind. One should, of course, avoid sensationalism and try not to twist the facts; and if one strongly argues a point of view one must also have defensive weapons against possible counterattack. But a proper slant does provide direction, and is very effective for organizing one's thoughts.

Relevancy means sticking to the subject, or at least not wandering too far away from it. Inexperienced writers tend to put down everything that comes to mind. Writing a research paper is like tending a tree: one must ruthlessly prune away all the wild growth to give it a strong, vigorous shape. (Let the first draft luxuriate, if you must, but attend to the pruning in the revision.) It therefore becomes a question of what to *leave out.* If your remarks have some direct or indirect bearing on the subject, by all means put them in. But if they just wandered in like strangers, and don't really belong, then leave them out even if (and this may hurt!) they

137

seemed like such brilliant ideas. The things you omit today may perhaps flourish in their own right on some other occasion.

Coherence is the connective tissue that holds a discourse together. Its opposite, incoherence, is alarming even to think about, associated as it is with senility, puerility, mental imbalance, and other sad conditions. Each idea must be presented clearly and move smoothly and logically to the next. This may be a matter of properly constructing sentences and paragraphs, or of making whole sections fit together. Assuming direction and relevance, one still needs the craftsmanship of coherence to make one's writing "jell."

181 Sequence of ideas

We put words on paper to communicate ideas. But the use of language is habit forming; when we are too lazy to think, we reach for an easy cliché or stock phrase which may not really convey the precise meaning intended at all. Therefore, do not plan your discussion primarily as a string of words, but rather as a sequence of ideas. Review each sentence, each paragraph, to see that the wording is transparent enough to let the ideas shine through. Language that is turbid (muddy), turgid (bloated), or prolix (long winded) induces boredom as well as misunderstandings.

Not only must ideas be clearly stated: they must move smoothly and logically one to another. Where a sentence or paragraph, or for that matter a whole paper, does not seem to "come off" (succeed), strip down the wording to basic ideas to see if the order of their presentation is faulty.

182 The brief

A "brief" is simply an extremely condensed version of the train of thought to be presented in a paper. It differs from an outline as follows. In an outline, one puts down only key words or phrases, in a coordinate-subordinate arrangement. In a brief, one must write short but complete sentences, each stating an important idea to be brought out. The sentences succeed one another as in an abstract (rule 170). In an outline, you leave yourself uncommitted; mere mention of a word or phrase does not indicate what stand you are going to take in relation to it. In a brief, with a subject and predicate for each major idea, you force yourself to take a stand. Admittedly, writing a brief can be painful if one does not know one's subject well enough to make positive statements about it. But it is excellent discipline, and there is no better way to assemble one's ideas and maneuver them into proper sequence. Also, it is far easier to arrange and rearrange experimentally a dozen sentences, for purposes of organization, than a dozen pages of text!

If possible, write a brief before tackling the first draft of your paper. But if this does not seem possible (and it is not easy), go ahead and write the first draft, then reduce this draft to the form of a brief, which is as much as to say make an abstract of it. This will lay bare the skeleton of the organization. Review this brief for any flaws in logic and for possible rearrangement of the sequence of ideas. The brief can usually be adjusted to make it more convincing. It is then used as a guide to revising the paper.

183   Expanding the brief

The simplest procedure for expanding the brief into a paper is as follows. Each sentence (i.e., positive statement) in the brief serves as a topic sentence for a paragraph in the paper. (See rule 188 Paragraph building.) For example, if the paper ought to contain about ten paragraphs, make up a brief with ten sentences, each suitable for a topic sentence. In writing the brief, one can make terse and positive statements, knowing full well that each statement will be explained at length in a fully developed paragraph.

In practice, this "simple" procedure is often modified in the interests of good literary style. A sentence that is quite at home in a brief may have to be reworded when it is transplanted into the paragraph it is supposed to govern. Because of context, paragraph prose differs in rhythm and flow from the prose of abstracts and briefs.

The same general principle can be used at different structural levels. Thus, a sentence in a brief might be called upon to govern a whole section or chapter of a long report or thesis. Or perhaps even a single long, complex sentence should be "briefed in" before you write it.

184 Opening remarks

To illustrate, let us assume a paper of short to moderate length with the first two paragraphs devoted to opening remarks. (Obviously, the opening may be briefer or more extensive, depending on circumstances.) The preliminary material is to get the reader's thoughts turned in the right direction before plunging into the subject. Opening remarks are actually difficult to formulate. After the rest of the paper is completed, always go back and review the opening. Typically, drastic revision may be needed to make it serve its purpose.

Extent. The opening should be the most tightly constructed part of the paper, because of the necessity for getting quickly into the subject. At the same time, you must write convincing prose, to attract the reader and put him at his ease. Actual extent will depend upon a proper balance between these two factors. You cannot afford to rush the reader; neither can you dawdle over long, eloquent pronouncements.

Starting point. To borrow the parlance of photographers, begin with a "pan shot" (full field) and "zoom in" on the subject. Back away far enough to show your subject in relation to one or more cognate (related) areas. Thus, if you are writing about one aspect of a thing, mention first its other aspects, even if you drop them in the ensuing discussion. One terrible mistake beginners make is to back away too far. Never begin with sweeping generalizations about whole fields with which you are only vaguely familiar. It is not necessary to burn down a house to roast a pig; anyway, the house usually belongs to someone else. For a starting point, back off no further than can be done with full confidence gained from your own exact knowledge and experience.

Standard opening. Assuming two paragraphs, devote the first paragraph to the broader implications of your subject, giving the reader a chance to get accustomed to your literary style. In a second (transitional) paragraph, work around to a more precise explanation of the task at hand. Define the subject and tell how you propose to deal with it. Explain important technical terms. If you like, give a brief preview of the layout of the rest of the paper, so that the reader will know what to expect.

Remember that the title stands alone as a kind of label, and is not a part of the text. Therefore, the text itself must introduce and elucidate the ideas contained in the title—usually in a paraphrased or restated version. By the time the reader has got through the opening remarks, it should be quite clear to him why you selected that particular title.

Dramatic opening. On appropriate occasions, try a more dramatic opening. There are two common kinds: (a) begin with a startling or paradoxical statement, which you are fully able to justify as the opening remarks proceed; or (b) begin by describing vividly some small, fascinating detail and go on to explain its relevance to the main subject. In either case, you take the reader by surprise in *apparently* departing from the subject as announced in the title. Naturally, by the end of the whole opening statement, the surprise opener must be fully reconciled with the title. In optics, the "paradox" opener is like one of those trick figures which looks upside down at first, but rights itself when you take a closer look. The "detail" opener is the reverse of zooming in: first a detail is shown, whose significance is not realized until we back away and see the full field.

Abrupt opening. The experienced writer who is weary of standard openings might try a more abrupt beginning. The very first sentence simply comes to grips with the heart of the matter: no fuss, no muss! This approach is more likely to succeed where: (a) the title conveys an immediate message requiring little or no explanation; (b) the subject is self-contained enough to dispense with "tie-ins" to related matters; (c) one knows *for certain* that the audience is made up of experts who will appreciate your not wasting their time with preliminaries. The method may also be appropriate for some narratives. (However, most narratives need preparation; that is, begin with background or a condensed synopsis, and start the narrative only at some point where it is really interesting.)

Opening quotation. This is one to avoid. The inexperienced writer, trying to get dramatic effect, is tempted to open with an isolated and unexplained direct quotation from his favorite author. Don't! It is ridiculous to present your title, and put in your by-line, and then start off with someone else's words. It is quite a different

141

matter if the author quoted is *properly introduced*. (Cf. rule 177 Opening a quotation.)

185   Paragraph sequence

After the opening remarks, paragraphs should follow one another in orderly sequence. Implement the suggestions already made in rules 179-183, and see rule 188 Paragraph building. Where there is a choice, shorter paragraphs are preferable to long, rambling ones. Each "new paragraph" provides a breathing space, and gives the eye a momentary rest. Where the flow of ideas has sufficient momentum, no special effort is needed to make paragraphs connect up—especially if they are short. But with long paragraphs, or where the complex of ideas necessarily requires a slower pace, transitions and connectives are needed. These are like couplers on a string of cars: they hold the train together.

A *transition* consists of a sentence or two for switching over from one train of thought to another. The transition may come at the end of one paragraph and prepare for the next. Or one can complete the train of thought and put the transitional material at the beginning of the new paragraph.

A *connective* is briefer: a dependent clause introducing the first sentence of the new paragraph, or even a phrase, or perhaps only a coordinating conjunction. (Cf. rules 191-194.)

There are times when a paragraph is purposely put out of sequence in what is called a *flashback*. In pressing forward with main ideas, the discussion may have omitted some of the essential background information. Take time out to provide such information precisely where it is most needed. In other words, the main ideas must be in proper sequence, but secondary and supporting ideas need not follow any order of their own; they may be interjected wherever they are useful. The wording must be subtly constructed so we know when you are going back to fill us in, and when you are returning to the main track.

The flashback technique can also be used, of course, for bits of information of less than paragraph length. *Caution:* Save the flashback for special effect; if overdone it would obviously make a shambles of your whole organization.

186 Sections

A report, term paper, or thesis chapter may be subdivided into sections by means of section headings (rule 29). Each section will normally comprise several pages. Section headings can be very helpful in revealing the organization of the subject matter; they tend to fix in the reader's mind the larger units of the discussion.

On rare occasions, *paragraph headings* may be preferred to, or used in addition to, section headings. These are more effective in printed matter than they are in typescript. A paragraph heading is indented with normal paragraph indention, underlined, and followed by a period. The paragraph begins immediately after the period.

Frequently enough, a paper (or chapter) can achieve perfect clarity without any subheadings at all. Do not use them unless they serve some real purpose.

187 Chapters

This rule applies only to theses (cf. rules 159-161); to divide a report or term paper into chapters would be ludicrous. The chapter title should provide a careful and accurate announcement of the content of the chapter. All of the chapter titles taken together (as in a table of contents) must convey a meaningful overview of the gist of the thesis as a whole. Indeed, manipulating chapter titles is an excellent way of controlling the broader elements of organization.

The various chapters ought to carry approximately equal *weight*, which is not quite the same as saying they must be of the same *length*. An average comfortable length is perhaps 12 to 15 pages—longer, if there is more to be said; shorter, if everything has been said. Where a chapter rambles on beyond the normal span of attention, the reader tires and his receptivity may decrease at an alarming rate. Each new chapter, on the other hand, induces a fresh burst of attentive energy.

For coherence, a chapter usually begins with transitional material. The link-up may be with the chapter just preceding, or with some earlier part of the discussion. Typically, the transition will recapitulate very briefly something already said, and use this as a point of departure for moving off in a new direction. (As a courtesy to the reader, actually *summarize*—do not merely say "see page so-and-so"!) Alternatively, a chapter may *end* with a transition—a brief foretaste of what is to follow immediately in the next chapter.

Any chapter opening ought to meet the following simple test: If I pick up the thesis and *start to read* at any chapter at all, will it make some kind of sense? Or will I have to plow back through all the preceding material to get my bearings?

XVI

COMMUNICATION OF IDEAS AT

PARAGRAPH, SENTENCE,

AND WORD LEVELS

A. Paragraphs

188 Paragraph building

Construct the paragraph around one central idea, and be sure that the idea is clear in your own mind before you begin to write. State the central idea in a topic sentence, and develop the idea adequately in the rest of the paragraph. Plan a smooth and purposeful flow of thought from sentence to sentence.

a. Topic sentence. The topic sentence will usually appear at or near the beginning of the paragraph. Where the central idea may prove difficult to grasp, write two topic sentences, one a paraphrase of the other. Sometimes, where a series of events leads to a result, or a sequence of arguments arrives at a conclusion, it is more effective to put the topic sentence at the end of the paragraph.

b. Development of the central idea. The paragraph development may consist in: (a) restating the topic sentence in a fuller, paraphrased version; (b) analyzing the idea in terms of its component parts; (c) illustrating the idea by describing specific examples; (d) giving the detailed sequence of events that led up to a situation; or (e) presenting the steps in an argument that led up to a conclusion.

c. Coherence. Avoid inserting irrelevant remarks that disturb the development of the main idea. Beware of facile words and phrases that seem to "write themselves"; they will usually lead you

145

off the track. Keep firm control over the wording and phrasing, so that these are at all times subservient to the thought to be expressed. Study the effects of rhythm and pace, in words and ideas, in order to give your writing vitality.

The relationship of one paragraph to another must be logical and coherent. There should be a smooth connection between the central ideas of successive paragraphs. (A simple test: Can an orderly abstract of the paper be made by lifting out only the topic sentences?) Where the flow of ideas is not naturally smooth, supply transitional sentences to guide the reader's mind in the direction you want it to go.

Paragraphs should be of an appropriate length—neither too long (stodgy), nor too short (journalistic). A good practical rule: Never have a solid page of typing without at least one new paragraph beginning. Conversely, avoid having more than three or four new paragraph beginnings on any one page.

B. Sentences and Phrases

189   Simple sentences

A simple sentence consists of one main clause only, with a subject and predicate. The subject will be a noun, pronoun, or occasionally a noun phrase (rules 194c, 194d) or noun clause (rule 193c). The predicate must always contain a finite verb, which may be transitive or intransitive, and in the active or passive voice. Strong, meaningful verbs tighten the pace of good prose. Overuse of the verb "to be" produces a vapid style, just as overuse of the passive voice makes one's ideas seem too weak to take any action. In short sentences, the verb may be enough to complete the meaning: *We all stopped.* But usually the predicate includes (a) material that describes the subject, or (b) one or more direct or indirect objects of the verb, or (c) adverbial modifiers of the verb itself. Naturally, additional words may be used to modify any element in the sentence. But as long as there is only one main clause (without any modifying dependent clauses), it is still technically a simple sentence.

When using a pronoun as subject or object, make sure that there is no ambiguity as to what the pronoun stands for. The "unidentifiable pronoun" is a sinister booby-trap. Check out all nouns within striking distance, and forestall any possibility that the reader's mind might jump from the pronoun back to the wrong noun.

Passive voice of verbs may be used (a) to turn the sentence around for better emphasis, or (b) to eliminate awkward pronouns, including the touchy first person.

The last movement *adds* a contrabassoon.

A contrabassoon *is added* in the last movement.

They performed Beethoven's pastoral symphony on December 22 at the Theater an der Wien.

Beethoven's pastoral symphony *was performed* . . . [etc.]

I found an example in measure 10.

An example *may be found* in measure 10.

190 Incomplete sentences

We are admonished to check every sentence to see that it contains a finite verb. No verb, no sentence—or rather an "incomplete sentence," like this one. As you can readily see, there are times when the verb may be purposely suppressed to produce a special kind of emphasis. Or a livelier pace. *Caution:* This device should be used only on rare occasions, when you know what you are doing. (Even then some readers may object.)

191 Compound sentences

A compound sentence contains two or more main clauses with no subordinate clauses. Two main clauses placed together without a connective are called *contact clauses;* they should be separated by a semicolon (rule 36—but see also rule 35). More often, *connectives* are used to join the main clauses.

a. Coordinating conjunctions are strong connectives such as:

and	but	for	or	nor	yet

These pull the main clauses closely together, and are preceded only by a comma. (In very short compound sentences even the comma is sometimes omitted.)

b. Conjunctive adverbs are weaker connectives such as:

accordingly	however	nevertheless
also	indeed	so

anyhow	instead	still
besides	likewise	then
consequently	moreover	therefore
furthermore	namely	thus
hence		

These call for a slight pause in the flow of ideas. They should be separated from the preceding main clause by a semicolon, and from the following main clause by a comma.

Note: As connectives, any of these words may also be used at the beginning of a new sentence, as a tie-in with the preceding sentence. In such cases, a conjunctive adverb is always followed by a comma. Distinguish between conjunctive adverbs and ordinary adverbs: However hard he tried, he could not succeed. However, at last he discovered the secret.

192 Complex sentences

The addition of one or more subordinate (dependent) clauses changes a simple sentence into a *complex sentence,* and a compound sentence into a *compound-complex* sentence.

193 Subordinate clauses

A subordinate clause must always have a subject and a finite verb. If the verb is omitted you do not have a clause, but only a phrase (rule 194). Subordinate clauses are used as modifiers, and may function in three ways. (For use of the comma, see rule 35.)

a. An *adverbial clause* usually modifies a verb (sometimes an adjective or adverb), and is introduced by a subordinating conjunction such as:

after	how	unless
although	if	until
as	in order that	when
as if	since	where
as long as	so that	whereas
because	though	while
before	till	why

In the examples, the dependent clause is in italics and the word modified in boldface:

When the singer missed his cue, the conductor **stopped** the orchestra and began over again. He asked the first clarinet to **play** louder, *so that the singer would be sure to hear his pitch.* "That was **better**," he said, *"because you came in on time.* Now the clarinet can play more **softly** *so that we can hear the singer."*

b. An *adjective clause* modifies a noun or pronoun, and is introduced by a relative pronoun: who, which, that (nominative); whose, of which (genitive); to whom, for which, etc. (dative); whom, which, that (accusative).

Some **composers** *who write avant-garde music* find that **audiences,** *whose tastes are more conservative,* resent **that** *to which they are unaccustomed,* and want to hear **music** *which they can "understand."*

c. A *noun clause* substitutes for a noun as subject or object, and is most commonly introduced by "that" or "what."

That we should search out every possible source of information seems obvious. But sometimes we cannot find *what we are looking for. What is most needed* are good reference tools, and we know *that such things exist.*

194   Phrases

In the use of language, the word *phrase* may have any of the following meanings.

A style of diction, as: long-winded phrases; a well-turned phrase; I do not understand your phraseology.

Any group of words that is able to make sense without a finite verb, as: good morning; no sooner said than done; out of sight, out of mind.

Any group of words (less than a clause) that functions collectively as a sentence element. In the examples, the sentence function is given in brackets.

[Subject] The *quick brown fox* jumped over the lazy dog.

[Object] We found *several different versions.*

[Appositive] Pierre Monteux, *the famous conductor,* died in 1964.

[Adjective] *Her eyes swollen with grief,* Helen picked up her typescript and left the professor's office.

[Verbal] The examples *could have been made* more intelligible.

[Adverbial] We run across these things *time and time again.*

[Conjunctive] *But in spite of these sad conditions,* one must carry on.

[Absolute] *The concert being over,* we went out into the street, *walking slowly along toward Piccadilly.* (Called "absolute" because these phrases modify the whole idea expressed in the main clause.)

More specifically, a phrase is a group of words introduced by a preposition, or by a verbal—i.e., participle, gerund, or infinitive. (See rules 203 Prepositions, and 199 Verbs.) Such a phrase contains neither a finite verb (that would make it a clause) nor a subject (it takes an object instead). For use of the comma, see rule 35.

a. A *prepositional phrase* is constructed with a preposition and may function as an adjective (the book *with the blue cover*), an adverb (he writes *in a clear hand*), or more rarely a noun (*without the pedal* is preferable).

b. A *participle phrase* is constructed with a participle derived from a verb and is used as an adjective: a man *writing a book* needs concentration; the symphony *heard last week* was better.

c. A *gerund phrase* employs a gerund derived from a verb. Gerunds end in *-ing* like present participles, but are used differently. A gerund phrase always functions as a noun: *writing a book* requires concentration; *meeting your father* was a great pleasure.

d. An *infinitive phrase* is introduced by an infinitive and functions as a noun: *to understand him* is not easy; one tries *to do one's best*; your aim should be *to achieve perfection.*

195 Enriched sentences

A writer with natural talent or acquired experience ought to feel equally at ease writing short, crisp sentences, or medium-sized sentences, or long and involved ones. This versatility is needed for the sake of variety and for control over pace and rhythm. In the first draft, keep sentences short so that the main ideas are quite clear and uninvolved. In subsequent revisions, the sentence structure can be built up, combined, enlarged as much as you like. Do not, of course, exceed the practical limits of intelligibility.

Having control over sentences means being consciously aware

of how they are built up. Starting with simple sentences, the following means of enrichment are available:

Compounding sentences. One easy device, often overlooked, is to bring two simple sentences together as main clauses in a compound sentence (rule 191).

Dual and multiple sentence elements. A sentence need not be restricted to one subject, one verb, etc. There may be two, or even more, of each sentence element provided the meaning remains clear.

The men, women, and even the children thronged into the square, stared at the colorful exhibits, and babbled and chattered in wonderment.

Adding modifiers. Important ideas should be described or qualified through the subject-predicate relationship of a main clause. But lesser ideas, or individual sentence elements, may be freely modified by means of words, phrases, or subordinate clauses. Test each sentence to see if it can be made more vivid, or its meaning sharpened up, by adding modifiers.

The man beat the dog.

[Words] The *exasperated* man *savagely* beat the *cringing* dog.

[Phrases] The man, *grabbing a stick*, beat *without mercy* the dog *in his flower beds.*

[Clauses] The man, *who had finally lost his temper*, beat the dog *that had been tearing up his flower beds (when he caught him at it).* [The adverbial clause in parentheses modifies the verb.]

Word chains. For special effect, modifier words may be strung together.

The long, tortuous, lugubrious theme rambles on insistently and interminably but finally and mercifully ends in a passage that is brighter, firmer, more intelligible, and on the whole more convincing.

Phrase chains. Phrases may be coupled together, either (a) to modify main-clause elements, or (b) to modify one another.

a. Musicians *of lesser reputation*, and *without any more secure income*, usually subsisted *in those times*, almost *without exception* and certainly *in the smaller places*, upon employment *at local taverns,* or *for wedding parties,* or *for an occasional concert.*

b. Those proficient on instruments *of the wind family* could participate in festive occasions *involving open-air entertainment of various kinds.* ["Of various kinds" modifies "entertainment."]

Subordinate-clause chains. Subordinate clauses may be cumulated (a) to modify a main-clause element, or (b) to permit one subordinate clause to modify another.

a. The performer *who has any sense of artistry,* and *whose technique is proficient,* studies a passage *until its musical meaning becomes clear* and *as if it were a challenge to his interpretive ability.*

b. The impatient performer, who is satisfied *as long as he plays all the notes,* may impress his listeners so that they think he is a genius *because they do not know any better.*

C. Words

For improvement of writing skills, keep constantly in mind the crucial importance of individual words. Where words are strong, vital, and packed with meaning they are workers. Where they are commonplace, colorless, and hackneyed they become drones. However skillfully constructed the sentences and paragraphs, they will fall flat without the support of effective wording.

196 Synonyms

Synonyms are words that have approximately the same meaning. Usually, though, there are subtle shades of difference. To increase your word power, make a habit of searching mentally for all possible synonyms for any word you are about to use. Select the word with just the right shade of meaning. Or, for variety, instead of using the same word over and over, alternate it with one or more suitable synonyms.

197 Parts of speech

Nouns and *verbs* are the principal agents of discourse. *Pronouns* refer back somehow to nouns. *Adjectives* describe or qualify nouns, while *adverbs* modify verbs, adjectives, or other adverbs. *Preposi-*

tions act upon a noun or pronoun to form prepositional phrases. *Conjunctions* are joining words. The *articles* (a, an, the) point up the application of a noun as being general or specific. *Interjections* serve no grammatical function, but are introduced for their expressive impact.

198 Nouns

Proper nouns (capitalized) are names of particular persons, places, institutions, titles, and the like. Common nouns may be concrete (names of objects), collective (names of groups of things regarded as a unit), or abstract (names of qualities, general ideas). Avoid capitalizing common nouns for emphasis; this suggests either a quaint, old-fashioned style or else humorous intent:

An eminent Bassoonist will play a Sonata this Evening; we consider this an Outrage. [Avoid.]

One often must make a subtle choice between capitals and lower case (a) for titles used formally or informally, and (b) for abstract nouns denoting periods, trends, or movements:

a. The program included Beethoven's Sonata, Opus 110, and Bach's Toccata and Fugue in D minor. In the audience were Prince Gallitzin and Countess Czernohorsky. The prince remarked to the countess that he detested the sonata, but that the toccata impressed him. [One could also have put, more informally: . . . Beethoven's sonata, Opus 110, and Bach's toccata and fugue in D minor.]

b. The classic period gave way to romanticism and, toward the end of the nineteenth century, impressionism made its appearance. [This seems preferable to Classic period . . . Romanticism . . . Impressionism; and certainly "Nineteenth Century" borders on the comic.]

199 Verbs

To split, or not to split, an infinitive (to write, to have written) may depend upon the emphasis desired: always *to write* it down immediately; *to* immediately *write* it down; *to* always immediately and carefully *write* it down [not so much "split" as cleaved asunder!]; *to* never *have thought* of it; never *to have thought*. The words that get in between are always adverbs modifying the verb. Split infinitives, once considered a serious misdemeanor, are nowadays viewed more calmly. But avoidance of splitting is always appreciated by discerning readers.

Besides infinitives, the other so-called "infinite" (unchanging) parts of verbs are participles (*writing, written*) and gerunds (*writing,* as verbal noun).

The "finite" verb forms indicate the time of an action (past, present, future) as related to a singular or plural subject in the first, second, or third person. Participles and infinitives may combine with auxiliary verbs to form verbal phrases: we *are going*; we *ought to have gone* sooner.

Verbs may be in the "active voice" (Dogs *chase* cats) or the "passive voice" (Cats *are chased* by dogs).

The three "moods" of verbs are indicative (indicating a fact, or statement), subjunctive (expressing a possibility, wish, or doubt), and imperative (a command).

Control over various verb forms contributes to both subtlety and accuracy of expression:

Yesterday, as we *were walking* down University Way, we *met* George. We *had not seen* him since the day he *was supposed to come* to our party. Henry asked, "Where *have* you *been? Come* with us!" George replied that he *had been studying* all morning. He *was told* by the teacher that if he *did not study* more he *would be failed* in music history. He *said* he *was going to study* more, but *wished* he *were able to remember* things better. He *could have got* a better grade in the last test; he even *might have got* a B. But the test *could have been made* a little easier. "Maybe we *can get* together tomorrow," said Henry. As we *parted,* George said, "I *am* sorry about the party. I *shall hope to be able to come* on Tuesday."

200   Pronouns

Personal pronouns in the first person (I, my, mine, me; we, our, ours, us) and second person (you, your, yours) seldom give trouble. But the third person (he, his, him; she, her, hers; it, its; they, their, theirs, them) is a potential source of confusion unless the reference (i.e., the common noun, or proper noun, for which the pronoun stands) is unmistakably clear. An *impersonal* third person is also available: *one, one's;* plural, *they, their, theirs, them.*

Relative pronouns (who, which, etc.) are used to introduce adjective clauses (rule 193b).

Demonstrative pronouns (this, these, that, those) must be distinguished from so-called limiting adjectives (this book, that flower). Where a demonstrative pronoun refers to a whole concept the reference must be clear: Composers, after writing several overtures, often turn to the symphony. *This* is to be expected. Sometimes a demonstrative does not refer back, but is immediately explained in an adjective clause: That *which comes easiest* may not always be the best; those *who think carefully* will agree.

A class of *indefinite pronouns* comprises a large number of words which may stand as subject or object: we have not seen *any;* as *anyone* can tell; *everyone* knows *something; many* would be satisfied with *either; no one* wants only a *few; whoever* comes late must take *whatever* he can get; *whichever* one of you broke it must pay for it.

Numeral pronouns are cardinal or ordinal numbers: *three* were given; the *second* was best.

Personal pronouns are made *reflexive* or *intensive* by adding the suffix *-self* or *-selves:* she bought *herself* a hat; we shall hate *ourselves* in the morning; I saw it *myself;* one must learn such things *one's self.*

The reciprocal pronouns are *each other* where two things are involved, and *one another* for more than two.

Interrogative pronouns are usually avoided in report writing. The exception might be a rhetorical question for which the answer will be supplied: *Who* came first? *Which* of these is best? *What* do we learn from a comparison?

201 Adjectives

Adjectives are used to describe, modify, or qualify nouns or pronouns, either as attributes (next to the subject or object) or as predicates (connected with the subject by means of a verb). When used appropriately and accurately, adjectives are perhaps our most powerful resource for developing a vigorous style. However, the force of adjectives quickly becomes depleted through overuse. One must keep constantly looking for new ones (cf. rule 196 Synonyms) and resist the temptation to use modifiers that are trite or colloquial.

An enriched sentence (rule 195) may, through judicious use of adjectives, be coaxed to do the work of several ordinary sentences:

The common transverse flute, with its three-octave range, is distinguished by the lyric quality of its middle register, the haunting, silvery brilliance of the uppermost octave, and the velvety, sensuous charm, despite its weak breathy quality, of the lowest octave.

Compare:

The flutes that are most common are played sideways. They have a range of three octaves. The middle register has a lyric quality. The higher notes sound brilliant, silvery, and have a certain haunting quality. The lowest notes cannot be played forcefully, and sound breathy, but nevertheless they have a certain charm that is velvety and sensuous.

202   Adverbs

Inexperienced writers tend to forget all about adverbs and their potential usefulness. Mostly, when we have found the right verb, we rush on to the rest of the predicate. But could the verb be given more precise meaning, or a finer shade of imagery, if we were to modify it adverbially? Adjectives may be similarly touched up by adverb modifiers. And, of course, one adverb may modify another adverb (quite happily; almost never).

Adverbs, adverbial clauses (rule 193a) and prepositional phrases functioning as adverbs (rule 194a) may be found or tested by asking questions:

a. How? Quickly, suddenly, slowly; he plays *without any expression*; she sang *as if she were choking.*

b. How much? Scarcely, equally, more, less, completely, extremely; he stumbles *more than ever.*

c. Where? He ran *upstairs* and stayed *there*; the books were laid *on the shelf.*

d. When? Often, seldom, always, never, soon, later, finally; they are coming *in the morning*; exits are to be used *in case of fire only*; I shall tell you *after I have read it*.

e. Why? We could not go *because of him*; we were *consequently* late; we *therefore* missed the best part.

f. Conditions attached? Yes, no; surely, perhaps, possibly, certainly, doubtless, absolutely; it is true *without doubt*; we shall go *if there is time*.

An adverb may govern a whole sentence: *First*, we looked for sources. *Unfortunately*, there were none available. *Later*, we heard there was a manuscript in the British Museum.

For conjunctive adverbs used as connectives, see rule 191.

203   Prepositions

A preposition (*pre*, "before," *position*, "placement") comes at the head of a phrase, to hold the phrase together and indicate its function in the sentence. (Cf. rule 194 Phrases.) English is rich in prepositions, both as single words and as word groups such as: according to, because of, by means of, due to, in place of, out of, up to. Writers' manuals such as those listed in the Bibliography give lists of the more common ones. Prepositions themselves do not give much trouble (as long as one understands the functions of prepositional phrases); nevertheless, one can renew one's vocabulary from time to time, even for these modest parts of speech.

Purists formerly dreaded ending a sentence with a preposition. But if the sentence seems less stilted or forced with the preposition last, then there is nothing to be afraid of.

204   Conjunctions

Coordinating conjunctions hold together individual words (ham *and* eggs; sudden, *yet* not entirely unexpected), or main clauses in compound sentences (rule 191a). Subordinating conjunctions tie dependent clauses to their main clauses (rule 193a). There are also conjunctive adverbs (rule 191b), which tie together the independent clauses of a compound sentence, or else a new sentence to its predecessor. Use any of these connectives accurately, so that they express precisely the relationship between the elements connected.

Correlative conjunctions go in pairs: *either* they are coming *or* they are not; neither . . . nor; both . . . and; not only . . . but also; whether . . . or.

205 Articles

The articles are *a, an* (indefinite) and *the* (definite). *A* is used before all words beginning with a consonant sound, including the "yoo" sound of some vowels: a book; a euphemism; a European; a usual thing; a yacht. (Also: such a one.)

An is used before all words beginning with a vowel sound: an actor; an element; an uncle.

Initial aspirated (pronounced) *h* takes *a*: a history; a house; a hummingbird. Where initial *h* is not pronounced use *an*: an honor; an hour.

Note: Aspirated *h* in an initial *unaccented* syllable may take either *a* or *an*: a historical account, or an historical account; a historian, or an historian; a hysterical woman, or an hysterical woman. In American usage *a* is preferred; British *an* may be a remnant of earlier times when such an *h* was not pronounced.

The may be used before singular or plural nouns. Omit *the* before a plural noun used in a general sense: Books are found in libraries. But include *the* wherever you could mentally substitute "these" or "those": the [these] books on the table; the [those] flowers in the [those] fields.

One may occasionally use the comparative form *the . . . the*: The more I hear Webern's music, the better I like it.

Nouns in a series may repeat, or not repeat, the article depending upon the shade of emphasis desired: a man and woman came in; a man and a woman came in; the toccatas and fugues of Bach; the toccatas and the fugues of Bach.

206 Interjections

In its simplest form, an interjection is any word or short phrase thrown in merely to express emotion: Ha! Bang! Good for you! What nonsense! Ye gods, how dull! *Alas*, it was too late. And *ah*, the sweet music that was made.

In a looser sense, one may break off a connected discussion momentarily to "interject" a passing comment, usually emotional or argumentative: The last three pieces are trivial indeed. *Why do they write such stuff?* They depend upon special sound effects that are by now quite hackneyed.

As you have probably guessed, interpolated exclamations are not in the best taste in formal writing. (In informal writing, whoopee! if you are sure of your audience.) Passing comments are more likely to take the less emotional form of "momentary digressions."

XVII

CONTROL OF LITERARY
STYLE

207   Literary style in general

If we stop to think about it, the flow of ideas through our minds during an average day is a chaotic jumble. Novelists sometimes use the "stream of consciousness" technique to exploit this characteristic desultory activity of the human mind. When we mumble to ourselves, or jot down little memoranda, the thoughts expressed are likely to be fragmentary and, to any observer, incoherent.

Ideas *can* be brought into focus, of course, as when we perform a task requiring concentration, or read a book, and so on. When we engage in conversation a further effort must be made: not only must we get our ideas in order, we must also communicate them. In any piece of writing, the writer is engaged, as it were, in a one-sided conversation with potential readers. Writing is more formal than ordinary conversation, and more permanent. It behooves the writer, therefore, to put his best foot forward.

The "literary" part of writing means the use of words and language to express ideas. Compare *literate*, as meaning "able to read and write," or as a modest way of saying "well read, and able to express oneself effectively." The "style" part of writing is really a blend of two things: (a) those qualities which, beyond the bare communication of ideas, induce in the reader a kind of aesthetic satisfaction; and (b) those elements in the manner of expression which give to any writing the stamp of its author's own personality. The corresponding strategy must therefore be: first, to arouse in the reader a glow of appreciation (even if subconscious) at the aptness and skill of the literary vehicle; and, second, to maintain the integrity of the author's own literary personality, whether unobtrusively in the background, or occasionally stepping boldly forward into the discussion.

Any creation that is well done and bears evidence of inventive authorship has *style*. We speak of clothes having style. Or the latest model of automobile may be well (or poorly) styled. Literary style, though, is not like clothing in the sense that one can lounge around all day in dirty jeans and dress up only for special occasions. Certain noted actors, in interviews, have explained that they work at their craft continuously, from the first waking moment in the morning until they fall asleep at night. Diction, bearing, and reactions to their surroundings are kept under firm control. The formal roles they portray are professional applications of this self-discipline. On stage, accidental lapses are unlikely, for they have avoided ordinary habits and colloquial diction. There was once a preacher who, to amuse his friends in conversation, often used the phrase "All ye feak and weeble sinners." One day, from force of habit, and without thinking, he used the expression in the midst of a solemn sermon! (Note: The unintentional or humorous exchange of initial sounds of two words is known as a "spoonerism," after the Reverend William A. Spooner, 1844-1930.)

The tape recorder is a handy device that enables us to hear ourselves as others hear us. For self-training, an inexpensive model will do. Practice oral communication with your tape recorder. The playback will give you insights, and encourage better habits of diction and style, which can be transferred to the writing process. Many professional writers, of course, have stop-go dictating devices, so that all of their literary composition is actually oral. It is up to the typist, then, to transcribe the material to typescript.

208   Diction

Singers will think of "good diction" as synonymous with clear and correct enunciation of words in a song or aria, whether in English or a foreign language. Actually, there is a more basic meaning applicable to both speaking and writing. Porter G. Perrin's definition is a good one:

Diction here means primarily the choice of words in speaking or writing. Good diction means that the words seem to the reader or listener well chosen to convey the meanings or attitudes of the writer or speaker; faulty diction, that the words either fail to convey the meaning fully or accurately or do not satisfy the reader's expectation in some way. . . . Very often the solution to a question of diction will be found by referring to a dictionary.*

209   Economy

Brevity is the soul of wit! And any writer who has his wits about him will attempt to announce what he has to say in the fewest possible words. This does not relieve us of the obligation of explaining things thoroughly. But explanations can be terse and to the point.

Actually, your text is a kind of cantus firmus against which the reader's mind is constantly weaving, voluntarily or involuntarily, counterpoints of its own. If your cantus firmus is long-winded, he will start improvising on his own, and his mind will wander. But if your wording is economical, he will have to pay strict attention, and you have got yourself a captive audience.

The "short paper" provides good forced discipline. The present author has used this device for many years in a training class in research method. In a typical assignment, it may take two weeks to do the research, but the student must report the results in two or three pages—no more! One quickly learns to sort out the essential from the unessential, and to search for means of expression that will not waste time. Then, when one tackles a real *pièce de résistance,* such as a long term paper or thesis, the good habits of economy already formed lend crispness and vitality to the style.

If upon self-analysis you find that your writing is "wordy," learn to wield an editorial blue pencil. Cut out words that contribute nothing to the meaning; consolidate material into enriched sentences (rule 195); for colorless and ambiguous words find substitutes that convey meanings more quickly and accurately.

* Reprinted by permission from *Writer's Guide and Index to English,* Third Edition, by Porter G. Perrin. Copyright © 1959 by Scott, Foresman and Company.

210 Rhythm

For music students, it may come as a surprise to learn that *rhythm* is an important element in literary style. They think they know all about rhythm. In music, yes. But what about in the papers the have to write? Poetry, of course, has rhythm—usually metered. Prose, too, has its own sense of rhythm, more irregular than that of poetry but effective in its own way.

Words fall naturally into patterns. If we inserted barlines into a typical prose passage, we should probably find a fluctuating meter, as: 3/8, 4/8, 2/8, 3/8, 5/8 . . . etc. Or even sometimes regular meter, as: 3/8 Where can we / find something / suitable? Careful examination might disclose other subtleties, such as upbeats and downbeats, syncopation for emphasis, triplets (in duple time) for speeding up, duplets (in triple time) for slowing down the rhythm. All forms of accentuation (tonic, agogic, expressive, and so on) also pertain to rhythm. Any sensible prose is bound to have its lesser and greater accents, its smaller and larger climaxes.

In rapid reading of prose we pay little conscious attention to such matters. But the rhythmic undercurrent is, or should be, nevertheless there. For an effective style it must be under some measure of control.

Each sentence ends with a full stop (period). Therefore, the only place we can control rhythm is within the sentence itself. Test your writing from time to time by reading it aloud for musical quality in terms of rhythm. Sometimes, where a sentence does not want to come off, the fault lies in its rhythm, which is out of step with the prevailing flow (rule 211) or pace (rule 212). Deletion or addition of even a single word may turn the trick. Or the sentence may need reconstructing so that accents will fall at the right places.

211 Flow

We are here reserving the word *flow* to describe the succession of *ideas* presented. To simplify, let us say that ideas come in different sizes: phrase-length, clause-length, sentence-length, and paragraph-length. These ideas should flow smoothly one into another, forming associations and groupings among themselves as they move along. It takes at least a split second, if not longer, for the reader to grasp each idea as the procession passes by. Some kind of suitable spacing is needed.

Fortunately, ideas come "packed" in words, and this packing material automatically spaces the ideas to some extent. In general, the size of the "package" should be proportional to the importance of the idea. For big ideas, let the words accumulate until they carry real weight. For lesser ideas, trim the wording according to the degree of impact sought. Occasionally, this principle is reversed: a big idea is exploded like a bombshell in one brief statement. The reverse, letting some picayunish idea monopolize a whole paragraph, is hardly recommended—unless, of course, your literary style gives the reader such aesthetic pleasure that he does not mind.

Test samples of your own writing by putting a mark at each place where an idea seems to crystallize. Are the ideas suitably spaced? Is the flow smooth and even, not jerky or distraught? Does the flow of ideas cooperate with sentence rhythm (rule 210) and pace (rule 212)? If the flow is faulty because of logic, reorganize. If the trouble is spacing, trim the wording around lesser ideas, and build up the larger ones. By "build up" we do not mean mere padding: you have probably left something out, because big ideas require fuller definitions or more detailed descriptions.

212 Pace

The pace in writing is rather like tempo in music. It should normally be *allegro* or *moderato*. Upon occasion: *lento,* for detailed narratives, or for broad concepts that require time to soak in; or *presto*, for rapid, staccato passages that can be quickly absorbed.

The pace, or speed, which you desire to set influences both the sentence rhythm and the flow of ideas. (Rules 210, 211.) If you will think about these matters, which probably never occurred to you, it should become apparent that they are powerful factors in the control of literary style.

One may alter the pace, just as one may have *accelerando* and *ritardando* in music. Or an abrupt change of pace (as in starting a new section or chapter) may act like a tonic upon the reader's attention.

A tight (brisk) pace is most often associated with shorter sentences. A sustained (leisurely) pace calls for longer sentences, such as the compound and complex varieties. If it helps, keep in mind the musical analogy: Fast tempo? Shorter phrases, with frequent breaths. Long, sustained melody? Let the theme gently unfold, gliding smoothly from phrase to phrase.

213 Imagery

When writing becomes overabstract, the trouble is that it lacks imagery. An *image* is precisely that: some visual, aural, tactual, kinesthetic, or emotional pattern or experience which the reader can call vividly to mind. Use of imagery supplements and supports the train of thought. "Sensational" writing draws heavily upon imagery, often titillating or morbid. "Dull, scholarly" writing, on the other hand, in its urge toward mastery of abstract thinking, sometimes squeezes out every bit of imagery as "unworthy." Some middle course between these two extremes seems indicated.

Writing that comes from the intellect must naturally embody much abstract thinking. But this can be liberally seasoned with appropriate imagery. Sometimes "one picture is worth a thousand words." There are times when even the most serious of authors might want to write so that the less well informed, even the man in the street, can understand. The broader public (and here I am tempted to define "public" as any one or more persons *other than the person writing!*) is better able to *think* when there is something concrete to hold onto, to feel, or to visualize.

Cultivate the art of evoking the right images in the reader's mind. Such imagery may be controlled through word association, illustration, or analogy, as described below.

a. Word association. Some words are richer and more intense in imagery than others. The evocative word triggers a recall of associations which may flash vividly upon the screen of consciousness, or may only surge up just below the threshold of consciousness. In the mature mind, vast quantities of verbal, sensory, and emotive data are stored in the memory. Take for example the musician who, when given the simple verbal cue "Chopin, Opus 10, No. 12," or the aural stimulus of the first few notes, can recall and "play back" mentally the entire Revolutionary Etude. For some, the recalled images are *eidetic*—almost as vivid as the original experience.

For others, many years of preoccupation with verbal communication may crowd out and subdue the other kinds of imagery such as the visual or emotive.

The problem in manipulating imagery is to employ a stimulus in *one* division of experience that evokes an image in *some other* division. Thus, music (aural) supposedly induces recall of emotive states, or even visual scenes. The sight of a flower brings to mind a line of verse. And so on. Writing, which is a verbal means of expression, ought therefore to seek its imagery in the visual, aural, kinesthetic, or emotive realms.

The *verbal-to-aural* channel needs special attention. In writing about music, we must frequently through the use of words try to recall what music sounds like. "The first theme appears in the oboe" is not enough. It tells us neither what the theme is like nor what particular kind of oboe tone is meant. "Theme" alone is an abstract concept. Suppose the reader has never heard this particular theme. How can he follow you unless you give him clues as to how the theme *sounds*? Each clue supplied (e.g., each aptly chosen descriptive word) brings him closer and closer to the approximate effect. The image you concoct for him may persuade him to go and hear the *real* theme. But if your paper is a dreary succession of Theme A, Theme B, second countersubject in the violas, with a half-cadence in C minor, the reader may only yawn and let his mind wander elsewhere. As for the "oboe": the tone quality varies, depending upon register, attack, dynamics, and so on. Here are some evocative words for "oboe" culled from two pages of an orchestration treatise: spicy; nasal; cutting through; poignant; gay; pastoral; not as agile as flute or clarinet . . . but speed and flexibility; legato; staccato; incisive; tiresome (if used too long); thick, coarse, honky (low register); ultra-reedy; primitive; thinner, less pungent; rapid single-tone tonguing; sensitive.

Remember, though, that the imagery must be appropriate and in good taste. Avoid expressions that are shopworn—e.g., "like little pearls." (This last is a figure of speech called a *simile*. Similes —where something is "like" something else—are dangerous, leading easily to an inflated style.) A final verbal-to-aural example, much too drastic to be used, may nevertheless illustrate the general principle: the violins squeaked, the basses rumbled, the horns hooted, and the trombones guffawed, while the big drum thundered a *pah!* to the tambourine's dry *oomp!*

The other channels, *verbal-to-visual*, and so on (to kinesthetic, to tactual, to emotive), are mainly cultivated to maintain an active undercurrent of live interest. The human mind so functions that the reader must inevitably and continuously supply his own commentary to your discussion. If you keep him busy fishing appropriate images out of his memory, he is not going to get into mischief. (Be careful of ambiguous imagery—the *double entendre!*) Example:

> The *craggy* castle, *perched* on a hill, *looked down* upon the *rain-swollen* waters *surging* between *reedy* banks. Jean, *fingers blue with cold*, grasped the railing of the *rickety* bridge and stared at the stream. Then he *turned slowly* and *looked up* at the castle, where lights were beginning to *shimmer*, through the *falling dusk*, from the *hollow-eyed* windows. His temples *throbbed* from the long walk, but still he must *pull himself* up the *winding* road to his destination . . . etc., etc.

This is too potent for everyday use. It represents a kind of literary "hard sell" where one must hold the reader at any cost. And yet this author has rarely seen a student paper, on any musical subject you like, that would not benefit from the addition of just a little more imagery.

Incidentally, since music is closely associated with eurythmics and dance, verbal-to-kinesthetic imagery can be extremely helpful in describing music. Assignment: *You* find some examples!

b. Illustration. Some advice was given earlier regarding illustrative material, both verbal (rule 131) and nonverbal (rules 132-135). We are now talking about the control of literary style, and specifically the use of imagery. If word association *evokes* imagery, then "illustration" in the sense here intended means the *construction* of an image, right before the reader's eyes, through the use of words. Illustration anticipates the reader's reaction: "All right, I think I understand what you mean. Now give me an example!"

When we summarize knowledge, define terms, or explain principles, our language tends to be abstract. But when we select a typical example and describe it clearly, the subject becomes more concrete. (Look up the adjective *concrete* in a dictionary.) Any normal discussion should alternate judiciously between abstractions (principles) and concretions (examples). Principles are best understood when properly illustrated. It is as though the reader had two channels of understanding: intellect and imagery. Switch back and forth between these channels, deliberately and with due attention to flow (rule 211) and pace (rule 212). This provides moments of rest, with renewed alertness, in the respective segments of the reader's mind.

In the following passage by Martin Cooper (describing operatic influence in Tchaikovsky's symphonies), the pace is quite brisk. There is scarcely time for "constructing" any elaborate imagery. But note the deft use of illustrations alternating with more generalized statements (here italicized):

> *The actual appearance of distinctively operatic phrases or melodies in the symphonies is rare,* of course, though in the Second Symphony Tchaikovsky did use a march from his opera *Undine* as a second movement: and very effective it is, with its purely Verdian movements. But *generally speaking, the operatic influence is more vague and diffused.* The opening of the Fourth Symphony, for example, is almost in the vein of a more sophisticated Meyerbeer or the Verdi of *Don Carlos.* The barking, hammering brass rhythms in the first movement of the Fifth, the emotional abandonment of the second subject, the voluptuous gloom of the slow movement with its repeated climaxes mounting almost to hysteria, the sudden brutal interruption, the pause and the return of the melody over the pizzicato chords in the strings—all these are devices of the theatre, or at any rate first learned in the theatre rather than the concert-hall. Even in the first two symphonies, where operatic influence is oddly less evident, Tckaikovsky shows a predilection for the sudden dramatic pause, the silence which is one of the most effective methods of focussing the attention of the audience on what is to follow. . . . Or he would use a brass fanfare to heighten the emotional tension, as in the first movement of the First Symphony.[*]

c. Analogy. A verbal illustration (example) is a sampling taken from the subject being discussed. An analogy, on the other hand, *borrows* material from some other field. Suppose we are writing

---

[*] "The Symphonies," in *The Music of Tchaikovsky,* edited by Gerald Abraham (New York: W. W. Norton, 1946), pp. 39-40.

about Subject X, and the sampling we select for illustration is Example *x*. But our example is weak in imagery; its attributes and functions cannot be readily visualized. Perhaps in some totally different field, Subject A, there is an Example *a*, with comparable attributes and functions, which is much more dependable for imagery because it is sure to induce vivid recall by almost any reader. If we present Example *x*, and follow it with what becomes Analogy *a*, we have a much better chance of being clearly understood. General principles may also be clarified by such borrowing: if Principle X is obscure, perhaps Principle A in some other field operates in the same way and is easier to grasp.

Suppose that I advise you, in writing a paper, to stay on the main trail and not go wandering up side trails; to avoid getting entangled in the underbrush of wordy rhetoric, and not to dawdle along the way lest you be overtaken by nightfall. I have merely borrowed the analogy of the hiker to suggest, in more vivid terms, the abstract principles of maintaining a sense of direction and a suitable pace in the composition of a paper.

Analogies come to us by inspiration. With practice, they may flow rather freely. One must develop a very sharp critical sense for testing their appropriateness. Faulty grammar, even a wobbly sense of direction, can perhaps be forgiven. But a misused analogy makes you utterly ridiculous. Warren D. Allen (*Philosophies of Music History*) devotes considerable space to the silly analogies of music historians of bygone generations. (Examples: Folksong as the "little wild flowers" of music. Or the bumbling, mathematical music of earlier composers flowing at last into the "mighty river" of Palestrina.) Not only must analogies be highly accurate, they must be used sparingly and saved for very special occasions. Taking a trip may provide a vivid experience, but overindulgence divorces us from the realities of the subject we are supposed to be writing about.

214   Figures of speech

We use figures of speech constantly, even in ordinary conversation. These devices of rhetoric (which is the art of expressive speech or literary composition) were already well known to the ancient Greeks. In the following list, classification and order do not

169

necessarily agree with what is given in rhetoric textbooks. Numbers in parentheses merely serve to call attention to eighteen traditional names.

a. Word association

(1) *Onomatopoeia* (from *onomatos*, a name; *poiein*, to make). Originally, in rhetoric, merely the use of words whose sound contributes to the meaning. (Cf. rule 213a.) Philologists pre-empted the term to denote words that imitate natural sounds. One may use normal vocabulary words, or artificially constructed expressions. Examples: buzz, hiss, whine, screech, gurgle, guzzle, plunk, thump, kachoo! whew! [a violent exhalation].

(2) *Metonymy* (*meta*, denoting a change of position or condition; *onyma*, name). Naming the cause for the effect, or vice versa, the sign for the thing signified, the container for the thing contained. Examples: we heard some Beethoven [meaning his music]; all the missing notes [meaning slovenly performance]; to address the chair [the presiding officer]; please pass the cow! [meaning milk].

(3) *Synecdoche* (*syn*, together; *ekdechesthai*, to receive). Closely related to metonymy. A part named signifies the whole. Examples: they had words [an altercation]; the strings [meaning violins, etc., not merely the strings on the instruments]. More rarely, the whole signifies a part. Examples: the city slept [meaning the people in it]; the war came to our village [not the whole war, but some local skirmish].

b. Comparison

(4) *Simile* (neuter form of *similis*, resembling). An imaginative comparison, formally introduced with "like" or "as." The given object, action, or relation is compared in one or more aspects with some other thing of different kind or quality. Examples: she sang like an angel; he wandered as in a dream; the themes scurried in and out like mice in a pantry.

(5) *Metaphor* (*meta*, beyond, over; *pherein*, to bring). Substitutes a description of "something else" which the reader is expected to apply directly to the thing being discussed. A simple metaphor is a compressed simile that omits *like* or *as*. Example:

these drunken rhythms stumble along for another six measures. Or the metaphor may be sustained for cumulative effect. Example: the composer saved his heavy artillery until the end, when he proceeded to bombard the audience with a barrage of brass and percussion that splattered incandescent fragments of sound into the topmost gallery.

Prolonged metaphor may turn into (6) *allegory,* where there is a whole series of actions (symbolizing other actions) with an imagined cast of characters. A *fable* is an imaginary narration to enforce some useful truth or concept, often with animals or inanimate objects speaking and acting like humans. A *parable,* on the other hand, is a brief narrative involving simple, everyday things and people but intended to convey some important moral or spiritual truth.

Do not mix metaphors. Example: from the scrapheap of outworn forms, a new form arose that blossomed overnight and spread like wildfire, capturing the hearts of all who were tuned in. [Horrible!]

c. Overstatement, understatement

(7) *Hyperbole* (*hyper,* above; *ballein,* to throw). Overstatement. Extravagant exaggeration for expressive emphasis. Examples: absolutely the most magnificent thing ever written; it takes him forever to make up his mind; I died a thousand deaths. May be combined with simile. Examples: as strong as an ox; Beethoven was like a colossus, overshadowing all his contemporaries. Or with metaphor. Examples: some modern art is sheer garbage; when a critic dips his pen in vitriol he should wear rubber gloves.

(8) *Litotes* (from *litos,* plain, simple). Understatement. Descriptions are purposely kept modest, or overmodest, in the hope that the reader will rebound sharply and magnify the statements to their true dimensions. Examples: a few people came to our concert [actually, there were several hundred]; London is a pleasant little town [sprawling metropolis!]; I have learned a thing or two in my time. Or statements may be kept modest to avoid censure. Scholarly writing is expected to underplay, rather than overplay— unless, of course, one can be absolutely certain, and hence explicit. Learn to protect your position with qualifiers: perhaps . . . ; it may be that . . . ; at least some of these. . . .

(9) *Euphemism* (from *eu*, well; *phanai*, to speak). Substitution of a milder, more agreeable word or expression for something ugly, harsh, unpleasant, or indelicate. Examples: she was rather plain [i.e., downright ugly]; the aroma [i.e., stench] of the city dump; ladies of the evening [tarts]. Clichés such as "he passed away" become so overworked that it is a relief to hear "he died."

(10) *Irony* (*eironeia*, dissimulation). Opposite meaning. A form of humor, ridicule, or light sarcasm where the words say one thing, but the meaning is intended to be just the opposite. Example: [teacher, to ungifted, lazy pupil] Well, I suppose our little genius practiced very hard this week? To avoid misinterpretation, give at least some clue as to meaning. Example: they played magnificently, considering that they actually got some of the notes right. In polemics (the art of carrying on a controversy), undiluted irony is a favorite weapon for infuriating one's antagonist, or making him look like a fool.

d. Arrangement

(11) *Climax* (*klimax*, ladder, staircase). A figure of speech in which a number of ideas or propositions are so arranged that each succeeding one rises above its predecessor in impressiveness or force. Example: interest engenders curiosity, curiosity leads to diligent searching, and searching sooner or later points the way to knowledge.

(12) *Anticlimax* (*anti*, a prefix signifying opposite). A succession of ideas, each of which is less dignified or striking than its predecessor. Example: at the age of eight he was a *wunderkind*; at eighteen, he still occasionally gave a concert; at thirty, he was playing in cheap back-street bars. The term "anticlimax" is often used to denote faulty writing, where ideas have not been put into proper sequence. When legitimately employed as a figure of speech, anticlimax must serve some evident purpose.

(13) *Antithesis* (*anti*, against, opposite; *tithenai*, to set). Opposition of ideas is emphasized by coupling the contrasting words within the same sentence, or by placing them in corresponding positions in successive sentences. Examples: the one was frugal with his talent, the other a squanderer. The Frenchman is a positivist by nature, and wants his art to show intelligence, craftsman-

ship, and taste. The German is a mystic, and expects inspiration, complexity, and depth of feeling.

e. Dramatization

(14) *Exclamation.* A sudden utterance expressive of strong feeling. (15) *Interrogation.* A question which, however, has the force of an emphatic affirmation or denial. (16) *Personification.* An inanimate object or abstract idea is represented as a personality endowed with human attributes. *Prosopopoeia* (*prosopon,* a face; *poiein,* to make) originally meant the representation of a deceased person as alive and present, or of an absent person as speaking. (17) *Apostrophe.* Where one turns from one's audience to address directly a person (dead or absent), or imaginary object, or abstract idea. (18) *Vision.* Some past or imagined scene or event is described as though it were actually present and visible.

215   Some faults of style

Here are a few descriptive terms to put you on your guard.

Academic. The criticism "too academic" implies a style that is more impersonal than it need be, unpleasantly abstract, aloof, dull, lacking in vitality, and so on. Otherwise, *good* academic writing is the preferred means of communication among scholars, teachers, and research workers, and is characterized by a certain formal dignity, scrupulousness in documentation, and serious attention to worthy matters. Academic writing is contrasted with the easier-going "popular" style, intended to instruct a broader public, and with the products of creative literature such as novels, plays, or poetry.

Bathos. From the Greek word for "depth," bathos denotes a disappointing letdown in style: (a) false pathos, or straining for pathetic effect; (b) subject matter or style that is dull, low, and commonplace, especially following in ludicrous contrast after something sublime.

Colloquial. A style suited for informal everyday speech but not for formal written communication. Dictionaries usually indicate which words and expressions are colloquialisms, slang, or dialect.

Dated. Inexperienced writers sometimes ape stylistic mannerisms of books written years ago—even whole generations ago.

Styles in writing change. Turns of phrase considered choice style in 1900 may now strike us as pretentious or comical. Good prose is ageless, to be sure. To be avoided are those modes of expression that have long since gone out of fashion.

Inflated. A style that is marked by ostentation and self-importance; pompous, bombastic, grandiloquent, high-sounding, tumid, turgid, swollen.

Insipid. Without any taste or savor; vapid, flat, dull, weak, uninteresting; wanting in spirit, life, or animation.

Jejune. Lacking any nourishing quality; empty and void of substance, interest, and satisfaction; barren, meager, dry, insipid.

Juvenile. In a pejorative sense: immature, underdeveloped, unsophisticated, emotionally childish, unworthy of an adult in vocabulary, subject matter, or intellect. On the other hand, effective writing for a juvenile audience requires special aptitude, skill, and experience. Educators and authors of "juvenile" books take their writing tasks very seriously.

Laconic. A style that is sparing of words, and also sparing in the expression of emotion or emphasis, in the manner of the Laconians (Spartans). A mild fault, which may be turned into a virtue when writing is brief, terse, pithy, concise, epigrammatic, sententious.

Malapropian (after Mrs. Malaprop, in Sheridan's *The Rivals*). Characterized by grotesque use of the wrong words. A mild example: when a student writes *Foreward* at the head of his thesis, meaning *Foreword*.

Non sequitur (Latin, "it does not follow"). Faulty logic, where the evidence given does not support the conclusions offered.

Obscure. Where the meaning is hidden behind a smoke screen of words. A style becomes *enigmatic* when we have to puzzle out its meaning as though it were some kind of riddle.

Purple patch. Sometimes used in a pejorative sense for a passage that is obtrusively ornate. The term is also legitimately used as an antithesis to bathos, denoting a passage distinguished by brilliancy or effectiveness in the midst of a work that is otherwise dull, commonplace, and uninspired.

Senile. Exhibiting the infirmities of old age: weakness, incoherence; mumbling monologues in a low key, or rhapsodic ranting at fever pitch; inability to grasp present reality firmly, and the seeking of refuge in outdated childhood memories.

Sesquipedalian. Characterized by the use of long words. The expression is humorous hyperbole, meaning words a foot and a half long.

Staccato. A staccato style can be very effective for short passages of special stress, but becomes a fault when overdone to the point of monotony. It employs short, rapid-fire sentences (often exclamations or interrogations), vigorous verbs, and tends to omit connectives between statements.

Telegraphic. A compact style used in newspaper headlines, and to some extent in the "styled" pieces in *Time* magazine. The essentials are present, but without the usual comforts of more leisurely prose. Telegraphic style is often ambiguous, as when we have to read a headline several times to grasp its meaning.

XVIII

KINDS OF WRITING

216   Audience

When a report is to be actually read aloud, as at a meeting or in a seminar, you will have a live audience. Even if your paper is purely for written communication, the audience of readers must be kept in mind. The potential audience may be very small, as when a term paper is read by a professor and handed back with comments. Or you might like to visualize a larger audience, as if rehearsing your manner of communicating as a teacher, as a lecturer, or eventually as a writer for publication.

Toward what kind of audience is each particular piece of writing specifically directed? Before you begin to write, take the time to form a clear image in your mind as to the nature of the group addressed. Are you more at ease with a select group of, say, half a dozen of your own contemporaries? Or if you visualize a larger assemblage of, say, a hundred does this provide a more resonant sounding board for your ideas, force you to enunciate more clearly and with better diction, and help you to adjust rhythm, flow, and pace to the reverberation time of a "larger hall," as it were?

How well prepared is the imaginary audience to assimilate what is presented? Assume that your auditors are intelligent and knowledgeable, but remember that they are not mind readers. If they are to know what you are thinking, you must tell them. You have the advantage: you have just come from your workshop (rule 179), where you have been devoting your undivided attention to the subject. They, too, may know something about the subject; but they have been busy with other things. You must give them a frame of reference, remind them of what they ought to remember, and redefine the terms upon which the discussion is based.

217 Technical writing

When a report is likely to appeal chiefly to a select group of experts, the writing may be uninhibitedly technical in tone. One draws freely upon the specialized vocabulary of the particular field, and sets a brisk pace, knowing that the readers addressed will readily follow the flow of ideas. In such technical writing, you must "speak the language" fluently, with complete mastery of the terminology, and with totally convincing presentation of evidence, illustrations, and conclusions. If you are not yourself a member of the select circle addressed, you must at least know all the passwords so as not to be laughed off the rostrum like some green apprentice.

Imagery (rule 213) may be geared to actual needs. For abstract subjects, very little imagery may be needed; any audience of experts is quite accustomed to manipulating abstract ideas. For more concrete subjects, the imagery of illustration (rule 213b) is approached, not from the point of view of a spectator, but as the expert himself would handle the materials.

218 Nontechnical writing

A wider audience will sometimes criticize a lecture or an essay as "too technical." This is a signal that the listener (reader) has not been able to follow what you have said. There are times when we ought to feel a deep sense of *obligation* to share our knowledge with broader segments of the public. On these occasions, one must be prepared to carry on a discussion in more general (nontechnical) language. This is not to say that the general public should be treated like children. Bear in mind that your potential reader may be far more competent in his own particular field of endeavor than you are in yours. He may even be quite experienced as a direct consumer of music, having attended operas and concerts, collected records, and so on. He has merely not had the specialized training necessary to follow a technical conversation about music.

In adjusting to a general audience, it is not necessary to pull any punches, nor to talk down to a lower level. Simply observe a few simple precautions:

a. Always include a *few* technical terms, but explain them thoroughly. The layman is always grateful for this; it admits him to the inner circle of the initiated, makes him feel wanted, and a bit superior to other laymen who do *not* understand these terms.

b. Keep the flow of ideas slow enough to make sure that your audience is always with you.

c. Complex ideas should be stated and restated in paraphrased versions. If we miss one wording, the next wording may convey the message.

d. Cultivate verbal description. In a lecture, you can always play a musical illustration; but in written or published matter, the general reader is not fluent enough to form an aural image by merely looking at a musical example.

e. Use analogies (rule 213c) much more freely than you would in addressing a trained audience. Some operating principle, or interrelationship of parts, which "everybody" understands may be the key to unlock the mystery of some complex musical process.

f. Addressing an audience of experts is more like a business meeting in a conference room. The general reader, on the other hand, you are inviting into your home, as it were. Put him at his ease, show him around, and make him feel comfortable. His visit with your subject matter is more relaxed if you occasionally interject some relevant personal anecdote, or rhetorical question, or describe how the reader might react in a given situation, and so on.

g. Finally, as a test of whether you are getting across, read your paper aloud to one or more average, intelligent laymen of your acquaintance. If they understand you, and are impressed, all is well. Or they may have some very good suggestions for improving communications.

219 Factual writing

In factual writing we attempt accurately to record reality, as existing in the present, or as reconstructed from the past. Reality comprises actual things, persons, places, events, circumstances, conditions, qualities, relationships, and so on, which can be directly observed, or for which reliable evidence is obtainable. The scholar is expected to assemble all the facts relevant to a particular inquiry, to present them clearly, and to indicate precisely where he obtained them. He may arrange the facts into some logical order, and he is permitted to make inferences and draw conclusions from the facts presented. He is not supposed to suppress any facts embarrassing to his inferences or conclusions.

One can scarcely avoid mingling some opinions with the facts presented. There is no objection to this, as long as it is perfectly clear what is stated as fact, and what is stated as the writer's or someone else's opinion.

220   Expression of opinion

Sometimes statements of opinion assume primary importance in dealing with a particular subject. This is notably the case in critical writing, where the opinion of the critic (whether valid or invalid) may be of equal or even greater interest than the thing criticized. Or when we read about events of the past, the account given may be tinged by an author's opinions, so that we have to sort out when he is telling the straight facts and when he is merely giving his own views of the matter. It is perfectly natural to have opinions; there is nothing wrong or indecent about them, and hence no need to hide them or cover them up in shame. It is simply a matter of asking oneself firmly: am I here primarily concerned with facts, or with opinions? whose opinions? are these the opinions of Jones, Smith, or Brown; or are they my own?

221   Forms of discourse

Students of music, by the time they reach the stage of seriously wanting to write about music, too often have forgotten the "forms of discourse" they are supposed to have learned during their earlier schooling in English composition. Traditionally, these are *exposition, narration, description, argumentation,* and *criticism.* An entire paper may be in one form of discourse. Or the approach may change as one deals with the various subdivisions of the subject, in chapters, sections, or even passages. To find a sense of direction,

179

ask yourself: Which form of discourse shall I pursue in this particular paper? or section? or passage?

a. Exposition. The purpose of expository writing is to explain. Simple exposition is the most basic form of writing to convey information. When the subject is difficult to understand, it is "exposed" by the orderly analysis of its parts and the use of typical illustrations or familiar analogies.

In a narrower sense, exposition may mean the first setting forth of the meaning and purpose of a piece of writing, an expounding of one's intentions.

b. Narration. The purpose of narrative writing is to recount a series of events in chronological order. The result may be a *narrative* (with incidental descriptive writing as needed), an *account* (less formal in tone), or a *recital* of events (with considerable attention to details). The main gist of the story (continuous, or in successive episodes) must be in correct chronological order. However, a skillful narrator can incorporate digressions such as the flashback, the anticipation, or descriptive detail without doing violence to the forward progression of the narrative.

Verbs should be in past tense, but may operate at different levels or "layers."

Layer 1: he went (completed); he was going (continuous action).

Layer 2: he had gone; he had been going (i.e., previously to the time of Layer 1).

Layer 3: on the day prior to that, he had gone (adverbial qualifiers needed to reach a still deeper layer in time).

One can also project into the future, as viewed from the time of the main action:

As he walked along, he thought he would go the next day.

Long before this, he had decided that he would be going there often in the future.

Mixed layers: When he had finished writing, after having been up all night, he collected his papers and went to the theater, where the play was to be given that evening.

Direct quotations should, of course, be in the appropriate tense:

As he walked along he thought, "I did not go yesterday, and today I am tired. I shall go tomorrow."

c. Description. The purpose of descriptive writing is to represent to the reader's imagination something which the writer has observed: an object, a scene, person, sensation, emotion, and so on. Synonyms for description might be representation, depiction, portrayal, delineation, sketch, impression, or characterization. The writer's task is to build up a careful and vivid image of the thing described in the mind of the reader. Incidentally, description need not depend upon adjectives alone. Often a verb, or a verb with an adverb, may serve an admirably descriptive function.

In most writing, description appears in certain sections or passages as a support and supplement to some other main form of discourse. However, a paper devoted to old instruments, for example, might be very largely descriptive.

The term "description" is sometimes loosely used for narrative or expository writing. Many, if indeed not *most* words have such different shades of meaning—now precise, now more general, now even ambiguous. In making a very tight classification (such as five forms of discourse!), meanings should be brought into sharp focus. At other times, the meaning is usually sufficiently clear from the context.

d. Argumentation. In everyday speech, the word "argument" often means a dispute, disagreement, altercation, or even wrangling and bickering. The true meaning, for use in formal discourse, is rather more sedate. To argue is to present reasons or evidence in order to prove something, to convince someone, or to persuade people to act in some particular way. Argumentation, then, is writing in which the process of reasoning is the controlling factor. The line of reasoning may be inductive or deductive.

Induction starts with individual facts that are observed or known, and proceeds to organize these facts in order to make inferences from them. If the inductive process is carried still further, it arrives (at least tentatively) at general principles or truths. A general law or principle thus arrived at is a hypothesis (a provisional conjecture) until it has been sufficiently verified by repeated testing to be considered a theory. Induction "leads upward," rather like addition; one assembles various parts to form a whole.

The opposite process of *deduction* begins with some general idea, proposition, or principle and proceeds to examine how it applies in specific cases. Deduction "leads downward," like subtraction or selection; one begins with a whole and drops down to a consideration of one or more of its parts. The term is often used in a loose sense: we say that Sherlock Holmes "made deductions," when in fact he made inferences from the evidence given.

One ought not entirely to forget the other meaning of argumentation: debate or controversy. The intelligent reader will very probably think of various objections to your line of reasoning. It is up to you to anticipate all possible counterarguments, to bring them into the discussion, and to dispose of them convincingly.

e. Criticism. The purpose of critical writing is to present the writer's evaluations and judgments regarding (a) the beauties and faults of works of art, or (b) the validity and appropriateness of actions or procedures, or (c) the style, content, method, theories, and so on, of other writers. The critic examines, judges, and forms an opinion. The resulting piece of writing is a *critique*, or a *review*, or perhaps a *critical essay*.

The just critic keeps in mind two frames of reference: (a) Are his own knowledge, experience, and understanding adequate for the task? Since judgment involves comparison with some set of norms or standards, does the critic possess a well-defined set of standards by which to judge? (b) Regarding the thing criticized, under what circumstances was it produced, and what was the intent of its creator or author? Has he accomplished what he intended, and was his intent valid?

The self-willed critic often pronounces judgment without full explanation of his reasons. But the wise critic, aiming to convince, mingles argumentation with his criticism, explaining how he deduces a particular judgment from a set of standards, and anticipating possible objections from readers whose tastes may differ from those of the critic for one reason or another.

XIX

WRITING FOR PUBLICATION

222 News release

Ayer's directory of periodicals reports for 1966 a total of 1,846 daily newspapers and 7,268 weekly newspapers published in the United States. Perhaps 10 per cent of the dailies are large metropolitan newspapers. The rest of the dailies and weeklies are published in cities, towns, and on down to the smallest communities able to support a newspaper. All of these publications absorb vast quantities of news and circulate it along with advertising (which keeps the paper going), editorials, special features, and so on. In the eyes of the managing editor, "news" is something the public will want to read about. In large cities, most of what happens locally never gets into a newspaper; space is available only for items considered newsworthy to the large public served. The smaller the community, the more likely that even minor local events will be read about with interest by the subscribers.

Newspaper editors are deluged by "free" material sent in by private citizens with something to report, or seeking to get their names in the paper. Most of this material probably goes into the waste basket. But, because reporters are busy covering their regular beats or special assignments, many legitimately newsworthy events would be lost to the reading public unless someone took the trouble to call them to the editor's attention.

The vehicle for conveying such information is the *news release.* Many organizations have an elected or appointed officer who attends to "publicity." This involves preparing news releases regarding the activities of the organization and sending them to all the various local papers in the hope that at least some of the information furnished will be published.

When you are involved with the sponsorship of a concert, lecture, or any kind of meeting to which the public is invited, see that all of the newspapers in your locality are notified well in advance of the event.

A news release must be brief, and it should quickly tell the information that makes it "news": Who? What? When? Where? Why? How? If paid admission, how much, and where can tickets be obtained. If free, include a reassuring "open to the public" or "complimentary." The reader wants to know what it is that is to take place, who is sponsoring the event, and who is performing in it. If you expect people to come, you must make it easy for them to find the right place at the right time. Give day of the week, date, and time of day. Or, if the time is not that specific, explain clearly. Give directions as to the place so that any member of the community who might be interested could readily find it. Special reasons for the event, if any, are newsworthy: an annual (or monthly, etc.) tradition or series; commemoration of a special occasion; in honor of some person or persons; to make available something to which the public seldom has access; to raise funds for a worthy cause; and so on. The manner of conducting the event may be of interest: a performance in costume; a lecture with film taken on a recent trip; audience participation; a recital upon a genuine Stradivarius, and so on.

Word count depends partly upon the size type used for the newspaper. In Newspaper A, a page has eight columns in 10 point type; one full column of solid matter (i.e., not counting headings and subheads) would run to about 650 words. Newspaper B has six columns in 9 point type, and a column takes about 1100 words. Translated to typescript pages, a full column in Newspaper A can take *two* or *two and a half* pages of double-spaced typed matter. For Newspaper B, this could be run up to three or four pages. The average news release, however, will be allotted perhaps four or five column inches of space: one must say all that one has to say on *one typed page.*

Several things may happen to the news release you submit: (a) it may go into the editor's wastebasket; (b) it may be rewritten by the editor or a rewrite man and published; (c) if good, it may be published exactly as submitted; or rather (d) for lack of space, the last paragraph or two may be cut off. In view of this last possibility, put all important things toward the beginning, and toward the end include only extra details that could be omitted without spoiling the effect.

As heading, put: FOR IMMEDIATE RELEASE. Or, if the news is to be kept confidential until a certain date, FOR RELEASE JANUARY 15. At the end of the statement, type your name, address, and telephone number; mention any official capacity, such as president or secretary of your organization, etc.

When submitting to several newspapers, avoid carbon copies if possible. No one wants to be "second choice."

223 Feature story

Unlike most straight news, a feature story or article carries a by-line. Most feature stories in newspapers are written by staff writers, or by free-lance writers, whose names are usually well known to the subscribers. Occasionally, though, an "outsider" is invited to furnish a feature story. This may be because the editor is convinced that the amateur can actually write well about his subject, or because of the human interest attached to a first-person account, even when the writing is below par.

The average feature story will run, say, to about 500 words. This would be the equivalent of about two pages of double-spaced typescript, *not more.* (Cf. rule 209, regarding the "two-page paper" as a way of life!) For the Sunday supplement, the feature story could be a little longer, but then one must allow space for good illustrative material. Actually, the editor who invites you to write a piece will specify how many words you are allowed, and the question of photographs or other illustrations should be discussed with him.

Editors of big-city dailies are much too busy to look at unsolicited manuscripts. The smaller dailies, or the weekly newspapers, are more likely to need extra material occasionally. Enclose a stamped, self-addressed envelope for the return of the manuscript, and a phone number in case the editor might want to discuss your contribution.

Feature stories about music and musicians, if you can get them published, ought certainly to help inform and educate the general public. Remember that you *are* writing for the general public. The story must be lively and interesting, should tell the reader something he will be glad to know, and may be more informal in style than the books and articles we had to read as college students.

Example A: A student went to Paris to study music on a Rotary fellowship; she sent several dispatches back to her home-town paper, which was delighted to publish a first-person account of goings-on in the French capital by a promising young personality already known to the townspeople through numerous recitals. Example B: A student, probing into the local music history of a city, persuaded the Sunday editor to run a piece about some interesting musicians who had been active in that city fifty years ago. Fortunately, there were some old photographs to be used as illustrations.

224 Program notes

The development of writing skill brings with it an urge to communicate with a public. Consider program notes as a readily accessible and satisfying outlet. Many concerts and performances are sufficiently elaborate to include a signed commentary in the printed program. Sometimes no one thinks of this possibility until the last moment; then whoever appears most willing is given the assignment, with only a few hours to prepare the material for the printer. The writer who has practiced this sort of thing in private for some time is more likely to meet the challenge successfully. Program notes may seem like a modest form of writing, but when well done they are appreciated by a very real audience.

As has been repeated over and over in these pages, *economy* is a vital factor in writing. The space allotted to program notes is usually limited by the cost of printing. If they are mimeographed, cost is not so important a factor. But the audience has only a few minutes, at most, to read and digest the commentary between the time of arrival and the beginning of the performance. The notes must therefore be concise, clearly worded, and readily understandable. (Opera synopses are particularly difficult to manage!) The writer must not only know the music he is describing; he must visualize how it will appear to the audience in performance. Piddling details that will not be heard are not worth mentioning. On the other hand, one may assume the role of critic, if necessary, to point out important features of the music and prepare the audience to grasp its main intent and meaning.

Do not fall into the trap of too much background, such as a long biography of the composer. One sentence is usually enough to identify the composer and tell what he is generally noted for. The second sentence might tell where and when the work was composed, or first performed, but the third sentence should probably come face to face with the problem of listening to, and understanding, the work itself. Where you can indulge in the luxury of lengthy program notes, put the essentials in the first paragraph, and let the reader take the program home and study it at his leisure for the erudite content of later paragraphs. (Speaking of erudition, Donald Tovey's *Essays in Musical Analysis* started out as program notes; only many years later were they collected and presented in book form.)

One tends to tire of writing program notes after a while. But they provide excellent experience and discipline and, after all, they do appear in print and reach an audience!

225 Reviews

Many periodicals carry book reviews, reviews of music just published, or of newly issued recordings. Publishers furnish periodicals with copies of the material in the hope of eliciting favorable reviews which in turn will stimulate sales. But the reviewer's function is that of a critic; his primary obligation is to inform the readers of the periodical, and he is not morally bound to "sell" mediocre or inferior merchandise. On the other hand, the reviewer wields tremendous power to persuade his audience to turn their attention to valuable and useful publications.

Periodicals usually have a reviews editor who either writes the reviews himself, or assigns individual items to persons of his acquaintance. To break into this field, it is indispensable to know an editor—or rather *to be known* by an editor. He will want to assign the review of a given item to someone whom he considers to be an authority on the subject, who can write intelligently, and who is likely to get the review in by a publication deadline. If the editor cannot immediately think of someone, he asks his friends for suggestions. If you are known to a friend of an editor, your name might possibly be suggested for a review assignment.

An invitation to write a review typically comes quite unexpectedly, with an early deadline attached. One must be prepared to drop other things and give concentrated attention to the task of reading the book, or studying the music or the recording. As for the write-up, one is not likely to be asked to review something until one has already developed some skill in making judgments and in writing effectively. There is nothing to deter the ambitious student, however, from writing practice reviews for his own amusement. This kind of self-assignment is strongly recommended as an auxiliary discipline to supplement other kinds of writing.

The other kind of review—i.e., of actual concerts, etc.—depends upon whether an editor is willing to assign space in his publication. Here, too, the "dry run" is good practice for the student whether or not he *ever* publishes a critique. (Cf. rule 221e.)

226 Articles

Let us assume that you have written a paper which you consider good enough to be published. First of all, get one or more responsible persons whom you know to read and criticize it. If your paper has merit, such persons may be able to suggest a publication outlet.

In any case, study carefully three or four recent issues for each of several different periodicals. You must have some clear idea, for any given periodical, as to: the kind of audience for which it is intended; the kind of material which it usually accepts and publishes; the usual length of article—short, medium, long. Unless your paper "fits" all three categories, there is no point in submitting it.

First send an *inquiry* to the editor: a brief letter, not more than a page, asking whether he would be interested in an article (for scholarly publications, a "paper") on such-and-such, describing the subject in one good sentence, and giving a close estimate of the word count. Another sentence or two may be added to describe some particular approach or method used, special sources to which you had access, and so on. If there is blank space left over, and if you enclose a stamped self-addressed envelope, some editors may immediately write an answer on the same sheet and send it back. This saves them the trouble of dictating a reply. If the editor is "not interested," make inquiries elsewhere.

If the editor invites you to submit your article, he should furnish you with a copy of the periodical's style sheet. In general, footnotes are typed double spaced at the end of the paper; illustrative material is on separate sheets; and so on. Type your name and address on the title page (upper left corner), and your name on each page. Mail in a manuscript-size envelope, enclosing a stamped self-addressed manuscript-size envelope. It may take *months* before the editor makes up his mind. Do not bombard him with follow-up letters! If you appear anxious, he will conclude that you want your manuscript back. A long wait usually means that your contribution is being given serious consideration.

Put the number of words on the title page (upper right corner). Average length depends upon the particular periodical. Let us assume that an average length article runs from 3000 words (approximately 10-12 typed pages) to 5000 words (15-20 typed pages). A short article would comprise less than 3000 words, a long article more than 5000 words. The word count is important, and should be estimated as accurately as possible.

Once an article is accepted, there may be another long wait before it appears in print. (A year or more is not unusual.) The publisher should furnish the author at least one copy of the issue in which his article appears. Some periodicals provide *offprints*—i.e., extra copies of the pages containing the article are printed and stapled together as separate units. Find out at the time of acceptance how many offprints are furnished gratis, or whether you have to pay for them. If, say, ten copies are supplied free, it may be possible to order extra copies (in advance) at a small charge. Budding young authors always like to distribute their offprints to all their friends. Experienced writers trade them (like stamp collectors) for offprints from other writers.

227 Books

The present writer once knew a student who became quite ambitious and wrote a book-length critical biography of a composer. He submitted it to a publisher, who wrote back that, yes, he would be glad to publish it, but that the author must furnish three thousand dollars to help defray the costs. This particular book did not get published. There is, however, a good deal of so-called "vanity" publishing going on all the time—perhaps not for music, but for all sorts of other subjects, where an author has some financial means and an irresistible urge to break into print. There is even a thriving community of ghost writers to do the actual writing, as when for example a busy executive or professional man has plenty of ideas, but no time to write a book which he wants published. Even authors of modest means may resort to vanity publishers for two reasons: (a) they hope the book will sell well enough to recoup the investment; and (b) they can get immediate action, without having to submit and resubmit to different publishers, and without having to make revisions to suit some editor's demands. Let us assume, though, that you do not have the money to invest, and that you would prefer to seek publication through more normal channels.

A publisher is not going to publish a book just to please the author. He is interested in books that have a potential "market" —i.e., will sell enough copies to repay the substantial costs of editing, printing, and distribution, and perhaps even go beyond the break-even point to return a small profit. If your book is to get published at all, there must be a *need* for it. The publisher may even expect you to *prove* to him that there is a market for your book, to indicate precisely what segments of the buying public will be interested, and what their total number will be. (He will also make his own estimates; that is his business.) A well-written basic textbook, for example, finds a more ready market than, say, a highly literate critical essay. Popular writing has a wider appeal than academic writing; and yet the publisher may expect very high quality in his popular titles ("trade" books) so as not to compromise his reputation. In brief: it is not the author who seeks a publisher; it is the publisher who is constantly looking for suitable manuscripts that would fill a need and that would reflect credit upon the firm that brings them out.

The two preliminary things an author usually does in seeking publication are (a) make an inquiry, and (b) submit a proposal. First address an *inquiry* to the editor of the firm you have in mind. The inquiry should be very brief. Ask if he would be interested in a manuscript (give the word count) on such-and-such a subject. If the editor is interested, he will ask you to submit a proposal. If he is "not interested," you must believe that the editor is an experienced person who probably knows more about books than you will ever know. If your inquiry has been clearly stated, he knows at once whether or not *from the standpoint of his particular publishing firm* it is worth while to go into the matter any further. Let us assume that the editor shows interest and invites you to submit a proposal. By all means submit a proposal first—not the entire manuscript!

When an editor calls for a *proposal,* he will describe very briefly what he wants. But it would perhaps help to spell it out here: (a) a title page, with your title and by-line, and any other information that is legitimate for a formal title page (plus your name and address in an upper corner); (b) a preface which, since it will have to explain your book to the reader, might also serve to explain it to the editor; (c) a table of contents by chapters in which, under each chapter heading, you include half a dozen subheads or statements which show clearly what will be covered; (d) a sample chapter or two, to show your literary style and manner of handling the subject. The *first* chapter is not the best, since it is usually preliminary in nature and does not indicate what happens when you come to grips with more involved aspects of the subject.

Thus far, you will not have been sending back and forth a bulky manuscript, but only letters and a reduced sampling. Before one goes to the trouble of writing an entire book, it is wise to find out if there is any likelihood of its publication. When an editor expresses an interest in seeing the *complete manuscript,* while this is of course no guarantee of publication, it is at least encouragement to go ahead and write the book.

Established professional writers may be able to obtain a contract with the publisher on the basis of the proposal. Assuming that you are not an established writer with a contract in your pocket, the editor will first want to see your complete manuscript, and he will have it read by one or more experts who not only know the subject but can be relied upon to judge the potential market. (This takes time, by the way. Allow several months before getting impatient to know whether your manuscript has been accepted or rejected.) If it is accepted, you had best do whatever the editor suggests from then on, and you will need no further advice from *Writing about Music*.

APPENDIX: SAMPLE PAPER

The following pages show a sample paper worked up from a brief (rule 182).

Title: The Influence of *Tristan* on the Songs of Henri Duparc
Brief:

The reputation of Duparc rests almost solely upon thirteen songs composed between 1868 and 1885.

Duparc was indebted to Franck, his teacher, but also has notable qualities of his own.

Purpose: to document the influence of *Tristan*.

What occasion would Duparc have had to be acquainted with *Tristan?*

Tristan was known to progressive French musicians from as early as 1860, when Wagner conducted three concerts in Paris.

The full score and piano-vocal score were available in 1860; Saint-Saëns, for example, knew *Tristan* by heart.

In 1869, Duparc met Wagner, and went to Munich to hear *Tristan*.

The Prelude was performed in Paris on November 15, 1874, and Duparc could have been present.

Give examples from the music (two paragraphs).

Conclusions: Duparc is at times strongly reminiscent of Wagner, but is not a slavish imitator.

Wagner is more contrapuntal and modulatory; Duparc achieves a serenity that is one of his strongest features.

THE INFLUENCE OF TRISTAN ON THE
SONGS OF HENRI DUPARC

By Marvin E. Reid

The reputation of Henri Duparc (1848-1933) rests almost solely upon thirteen songs composed between 1868 and 1885. The belated publication of the songs gives a false idea of the date of their actual composition. Over-critical of his own work, Duparc destroyed a number of instrumental compositions, though the symphonic poem Lénore (1875) survives, and is thought by some to be an excellent example of this genre. The composer took an active interest in developments in French music up to 1885, when illness forced him to abandon composition and retire to Switzerland.[1] Becoming increasingly blind and paralytic, he found refuge in religion and prayer.[2]

Sidney Northcote, writing in 1932, acknowledges Duparc's debt to César Franck, his teacher, but finds in the songs "a more positive melodic eloquence" than Franck ever achieved. The harmonic texture of Duparc's songs is described as

> always fluid and expressive, with a sincere impressionism that is at once restrained and expressive. There is a quality of originality in the flexibility and amplitude of phrase and development, and the sincerity and balance of the poetic declamation are undeniable. Without

---

1 Marie Louise Pereyra, "Duparc," Grove's Dictionary of Music and Musicians (3rd edn., 1927), II, 114. Mlle Pereyra mentions "15 songs." Her article was revised by Sidney Northcote for the 5th edn. (1954), II, 811-12, where 16 songs and a duo are listed. See also the Appendix to this paper.

2 Gérard Souzay, jacket notes for Songs by Henri Duparc (Philips PHM 500-027). See also Edward Lockspeiser, who mentions Duparc's talent as an amateur painter. (The Music Masters, III, 114-17.)

doubt, he was deeply indebted to his friend Castillon, whose "Six Poésies" (Op. 8) mark the essential source of an impulse that passed through Duparc and Chausson down to contemporary French song. 3

Wagner's influence upon French composers of the later nineteenth century is often mentioned, and it is the purpose of the present paper to document, at least speculatively, the possible influence specifically of Tristan upon the songs of Henri Duparc. Northcote mentions the "obvious influence of Liszt and Wagner."[4] Martin Cooper suggests that Duparc's natural lyrical gift may be seen, for example, in the opening of Chanson triste, which he calls "the contemporary drawing-room romance at its very best."

> What that lyrical gift would become when enriched and made more subtle by a thorough assimilation of Wagnerian harmony can be seen in a single passage later in the same song: "Tu prendras ma tête malade, Oh! quelque-fois sur tes genoux," . . . or in a whole song like L'Invitation au voyage, Extase or Soupir. Enharmony is at the root of Duparc's style, but enharmony in the Lisztian sense . . . or, even more frequent, in the manner of Tristan. . . ." 5

A question that comes to mind is: What occasion would Duparc have had to be acquainted with the score of Tristan? The opera, it will be recalled had its first performance in Munich, on June 10, 1865, and supposedly was not given in Paris until October 28, 1899 (at the Nouveau Théâtre).[6]

Actually, Tristan was known to progressive French musicians from as early as 1860. On three successive Wednesdays of that year--January 25, February 1 and 8--Wagner conducted three concerts of his own works. The hall (the Salle Ventadour), seating about 1550, was rented for the occasion, plunging Wagner further into debt. The program, virtually the same at all three concerts, included besides selections from The

---

3 Sidney Northcote, "The Songs of Henri Duparc," Music and Letters, XIII (1932), 401-4.
4 Ibid., p. 402.
5 Martin Cooper, French Music from the Death of Berlioz to the Death of Fauré (Oxford University Press, 1951), pp. 62-63.
6 Stéphane Wolff, L'Opéra au Palais Garnier (1875-1962), p. 214.

Flying Dutchman, Tannhäuser, and Lohengrin the Prelude to Tristan with
Wagner's concert ending.[7] Whether Henri Duparc was in the audience,
I do not know; he would have been a boy of twelve.

The full score of Tristan was published by Breitkopf & Härtel in
1860, as was also Bülow's piano-vocal reduction.[8] In mid-January, 1860,
Wagner presented an advance copy of the full score to Berlioz.[9]
"Saint-Saëns, then only twenty-five," says Newman, "impressed Wagner by
his technical assurance, especially his facility in score-reading. In
those days Saint-Saëns was an ardent Wagnerite: Wagner was astonished
to find that he knew Tristan by heart."[10] Another "ardent admirer" was
Gounod, to whom Wagner gave a full score of Tristan in 1861 before he
left Paris.[11] It is reasonable to suppose that copies of the piano-vocal
score would have circulated rather freely among the Parisian "Wagnerites"
in the 1860's.

Northcote mentions Duparc's close association with Saint-Saëns, who
at this time was a Liszt enthusiast. It is implied that Duparc also knew
Liszt, for it was at his house in Weimar in 1869 that he met Wagner.[12]
In 1869, Duparc went with D'Indy to Munich to hear Tristan and Rheingold,
and in 1870 he went again for Die Walküre.[13] There is reason to believe
that Extase (1878) was written deliberately in Tristan style either to
upset or to convince the anti-Wagnerian critics.[14]

Vallas relates an anecdote regarding Vincent D'Indy, who attended a
Pasdeloup concert on November 15, 1874, where the Prelude to Tristan was

---

7 Ernest Newman, The Life of Richard Wagner, III, 5-6. The dates are
confirmed by Emerich Kastner, Wagner-Catalog (1878), pp. 50-51.
8 Kastner, Wagner-Catalog, p. 47.
9 Newman, III, 15.
10 Ibid., p. 11.   11 Ibid., p. 11.
12 Sidney Northcote, The Songs of Henri Duparc (London: Dobson, 1949),
pp. 46-47.
13 Ibid., p. 43.   14 Ibid., p. 47.

performed. (This is mistakenly called the first performance in France!)
The enthusiasm of the eighteen "Wagnerites" present was drowned by the
indifference of the audience as a whole. But the Prelude was repeated at
the end of the concert after the departure of the anti-Wagnerites.[15]
The seventeen, other than D'Indy, are not named; but it is plausible, in
view of his association with D'Indy, that Duparc was among the group.[16]

For internal evidence, one can turn to the songs themselves.[17]
The opening of L'Invitation au voyage (Example 1) has a kind of Wagnerian
resonance with its French-sixth chords (F^6) and "Wagnerian" seventh-
chord (W^7). Wagner, though, is more likely to resolve a French sixth to
a dominant seventh. (Example 2.)

Example 1. Duparc, L'Invitation au voyage, meas. 1-9, harmonic synopsis.

Example 2. Wagner, Tristan: (a) Prelude, meas. 36-37;
(b) Act I, sc. ii, meas. 28-30.

15 Léon Vallas, Vincent D'Indy (Paris: Michel, 1946), I, 199-200.
16 See Vallas' index, with 56 page references to Duparc.
17 Henri Duparc, Mélodies (Paris: Rouart, Lerolle, c1911), 77 p.
Subtitled "Nouvelle édition complète," with thirteen songs.

In Extase, the chromatic ascending line (meas. 1-2) and appoggiaturas
(meas. 3-4) have a Wagnerian sound. Measure 4 is redolent of the sonority
of Isolde's first "Liebe" in the Liebestraum scene (Act II, sc. ii, Mässig
langsam, meas. 12-13). Wagner's striking Death motive (Act I, sc. ii,
meas. 24-27) has a characteristic progression from a 6-chord (A flat) to a
triad (A) with the real root moving up a semitone. Duparc achieves a comparable effect in Extase with real roots progressing up a tritone (meas.
10-11, and 12-13).

An admittedly hurried perusal of the thirteen songs and the piano-
vocal score of Tristan leads the present writer to the following tentative
conclusions: Duparc is at times--often fleetingly so--strongly reminiscent
of Tristan. It is inconceivable that a composer could write in this style
without having been saturated in the "sound" of Wagner. At the same time,
some of Duparc's most Wagnerian-sounding harmonic progressions turn out
different from "corresponding" places in Tristan. It is as though Duparc
had assimilated the idea, the essence, and devised his own technical means
for achieving comparable expression.

Much of Wagner's texture involves interweaving contrapuntal strands
and constant modulation. Duparc avoids counterpoint; at best one finds an
occasional fragment of countermelody in the accompaniment. And, because
these are songs--not music drama--Duparc is essentially stable tonally;
harmonic shifts lend color rather than genuinely modulatory propulsion.
With all his depth of expression, Duparc achieves a serenity (thanks
largely to his style of declamation) that justifies the artistic validity
of these works. It is a serenity comparable with the Liebestraum of
Tristan and Isolde, expressed with restraint, with Gallic originality,
and the fine, sharp lines of charming miniatures.

APPENDIX

Chronological List of the Songs of Henri Duparc

Poets are given in parentheses. Bracketed numbers indicate the order in the Rouart Lerolle edition of 1911. "orch" indicates that the original version was with orchestra. "also orch" indicates a piano-voice original that was later orchestrated by Duparc.

*[1868   Sérénade (Gabriel Marc)]

*[1868   Romance de Mignon (trans. from Goethe)]

1868   Le Galop (Sully-Prudhomme) reissued by Durand, 1948

1868   Chanson triste (Jean Lahor) also orch [No. 9]

1868   Soupir (Sully-Prudhomme) [No. 11]

1869   Au Pays où se fait la guerre (Théophile Gautier) also orch [No. 13]

1870   L'Invitation au voyage (Charles Baudelaire) also orch [No. 1]

1871   La Vague et la cloche (François Coppée) orch [No. 3]

**[1872   La Fuite, duo for soprano and tenor (Théophile Gautier)]

1874   Élégie (trans. from Thomas Moore) [No. 10]

1878   Extase (Jean Lahor) [No. 4]

1879   Le Manoir de Rosemonde (Robert de Bonnières) [No. 6]

1880   Sérénade florentine (Jean Lahor) [No. 2]

1882   Phidylé (Leconte de Lisle) also orch [No. 5]

1883   Testament (Armand Silvestre) also orch [No. 8]

1883   Lamento (Théophile Gautier) [No. 7]

1884   La Vie antérieure (Charles Baudelaire) orch [No. 12]

* "Suppressed" according to Northcote (1949), but listed in Grove (5th edn., 1954).

** "Destroyed" according to Northcote (1949), but listed in Grove (5th edn., 1954).

The Rouart Lerolle edition states that all songs were originally for high voice excepting Nos. 8 and 12 (medium voice) and No. 3 (low voice).

7

BIBLIOGRAPHY

Cooper, Martin. French Music from the Death of Berlioz to the Death
of Fauré. London: Oxford University Press, 1951. 239 p.

Duparc, Henri. Mélodies: Nouvelle édition complète.
Paris: Louart, Lerolle, c1911. 77 p.

-------. Songs by Henri Duparc. Gérard Souzay, baritone; Dalton
Baldwin, pianist. Philips PHM 500-027. Jacket notes by Gérard
Souzay.

Kastner, Emerich. Wagner-Catalog: Chronologisches Verzeichniss der
von und über Richard Wagner erschienenen Schriften, Musikwerke, etc.
Offenbach, 1878. Reprinted, Hilversum: Frits Knuf, 1966. 181 p.

Lockspeiser, Edward. "Henri Duparc," in The Romantic Age, pp. 114-17.
(The Music Masters, Vol. III.) Penguin Books, 1958.

Newman, Ernest. The Life of Richard Wagner. 4 vols. New York:
Knopf, 1933-1946.

Northcote, Sidney. "The Songs of Henri Duparc," Music and Letters,
XIII (1932), 401-4.

-------. The Songs of Henri Duparc. London: Dobson, 1949. 122 p.

Pereyra, Marie Louise. "Duparc," Grove's Dictionary of Music and
Musicians. Third edition, edited by H. C. Colles. New York:
Macmillan, 1927. (Vol. II, p. 114.) Also, with additions by
Sidney Northcote, in the Fifth edition, edited by Eric Blom.
New York: St. Martin's Press, 1954. (Vol. II, pp. 511-12.)

Vallas, Léon. Vincent D'Indy. 2 vols. Paris: Michel, 1946.

Wagner, Richard. Tristan und Isolde. Klavierauszug mit Text, von
Mottl u. Kogel. Leipzig: Peters, n.d. 321 p.
(Peters Edition No. 3407, with publisher's plate no. 9815; Felix
Mottl died in 1911, and Gustav Kogel in 1921.)

Wolff, Stéphane. L'Opéra au Palais Garnier (1875-1962).
Paris: l'Entr'acte, n.d. 565 p.

BIBLIOGRAPHY

STYLE MANUALS FOR PUBLICATION

A Manual of Style. Containing typographical and other rules for authors, printers, and publishers recommended by the University of Chicago Press, together with specimens of type. 11th edition. Chicago: The University of Chicago Press [11030 South Langley Avenue, Chicago, Illinois 60628], 1949. x, 534 p. The standard reference work, with detailed information on all aspects of preparing books for publication. Rules for preparation of copy, pp. 23-187; hints to authors, editors, and proofreaders, pp. 191-231; glossary of technical terms, pp. 245-272; specimens of type, pp. 280-467. See also the 12th ed., 1968.

The MLA Style Sheet. Revised edition. Compiled by William Riley Parker. New York: The Modern Language Association of America [4 Washington Place, New York, N.Y. 10003], 1961. 30 p. A practical compendium of style acceptable to any of eighty journals and twenty-eight university presses. With Supplement on the preparation of master's and doctor's theses, pp. 24-25.

STUDENT MANUALS FOR TYPESCRIPT

The following inexpensive manuals, though not applying specifically to music, contain many helpful hints on a great variety of matters. Note that *Writing about Music* disagrees with them on certain details, such as indention and footnote form.

Kate L. Turabian. *A Manual for Writers of Term Papers, Theses and Dissertations.* Chicago: University of Chicago Press, 1955. Paperback edition (Phoenix Books), 1960. vii, 110 p.

Edward D. Seeber. *A Style Manual for Students Based on the MLA Style Sheet.* Bloomington: Indiana University Press, 1964. Paperback (A Midland Book). 94 p.

WRITER'S GUIDES

Porter G. Perrin. *Writer's Guide and Index to English.* Third edition. Revised with the assistance of Karl W. Dykema. Chicago: Scott, Foresman and Company, 1959. 816 p. Superior in literary style, and recommended as a constant companion for any writer. Part I, "Writer's Guide," pp. 3-400, contains chapters on varieties of English, spelling, punctuation, paragraphs, sentences, words and phrases, stages in writing, and various kinds of papers, with specimen pages. Part II, "Index to English," pp. 401-770, is a kind of alphabetical encyclopedia of helpful information.

Archibald C. Jordan. *The Writer's Manual: The Grammar and Mechanics of the English Language.* Cleveland: World Publishing Company, 1966. 387 p.

Highly recommended for students needing a basic and systematic review of grammar and writing skills.

John C. Hodges. *Harbrace College Handbook.* Fifth edition. New York: Harcourt, Brace and World, 1962. 502 p. Organized for quick reference to detail matters within any of thirty-five major principles of effective writing.

METHODS AND MATERIALS OF RESEARCH IN MUSIC

Ruth T. Watanabe. *Introduction to Music Research.* Englewood Cliffs, N.J.: Prentice-Hall, 1967. 237 p. By a distinguished music librarian, this book is especially helpful as a guide to bibliography. Sections on library orientation, the research paper, and survey of research materials.

INDEX

Theses (as sources of information): footnote references to, 66; bibliography entries for, 94

Theses (as writing projects): outline for, 5; variable regulations for, 11; title page for, 18, 118; submitted unbound, 117; arrangement of content in, 117-18; table of contents in, 118; other lists in, 118-19; preface in, 119; acknowledgments in, 119-20; chapters in, 120-22; arrangement other than by chapters in, 122; appendix in, 122; glossary in, 123; cumulated musical examples in, 123; index for, 123; formulation of title for, 136-37; chapters in, 143-44

Title page: for term paper or thesis, 18, 117, 118; of books, as source of information, 77, 81, 82, 84

Titles: main, 19, 21, 25, 28, 136-37; for book review, 20; references to in text, 27, 98-99; cited in footnote, 55-69 *passim;* entered in bibliography, 77-96 *passim;* treated as verbal matter, 103

Topic sentence, 6, 145

Transition: between paragraphs, 142; between chapters, 143-44

Translation: parenthetical, 26, 79; cited as reference, 81, 84, 85; of quotations, 134-35

Type: faces, 12-13; reduction of, 16-17; sizes of, 116

Typescript: definition of, 4; as fair copy, 8; preliminary preparations for, 10; appearance of, 11; end pages in, 18

Umlaut: symbol for, 14; in German, 37

Underlining: symbol for, 14; of published works, 19, 28, 98-99; of foreign words, 19, 28, 36, 37, 43; for emphasis, 28, 36; of word being discussed, 28, 29, 36

Unpublished material. *See* Manuscript sources; Recordings; Theses (as sources of information)

Verbal examples, 102-3

Verbs: spelling of, 34; in simple sentence, 146-47; form, voice, and mood of, 153-54

Verifax, 112

Virgule. *See* Slant line

Vocabulary. *See* Glossary

Volumes: abbreviations for, 47, 49, 100; of periodicals, 56, 86; in a series, 59, 85-86, 89, 90-91

Words: compound, 25; contractions of, 28; being discussed in text, 28-29

Xerox process: reproducing musical examples, 104, 110-11; explanation of, 109-10; reproducing from microfilm, 113. *See also* Photocopying processes

Years, inclusive, 31-32